MONTEREY, CARMEL,
BIG SUR, SANTA CRUZ

Weekend
Adventure
getaways

MONTEREY
CARMEL, BIG SUR
SANTA CRUZ

RICHARD HARRIS

PHOTOGRAPHY BY **LEE FOSTER**

Ulysses Press

Published by:
Ulysses Press
P.O. Box 3440
Berkeley, CA 94703
www.ulyssespress.com

ISBN 1-56975-385-7
ISSN 1545-5637

Printed in Canada by Transcontinental Printing
10 9 8 7 6 5 4 3 2 1

Front cover photography: © gettyimages.com
Back cover photography: Lee Foster
Design: Sarah Levin, Leslie Henriques
Editorial and production: Claire Chun, Lily Chou, Steven Schwartz
Maps: Pease Press
Index: Sayre Van Young

Distributed in the United States by Publishers Group West
and in Canada by Raincoast Books

Ulysses Press 🐢 is a federally registered trademark of BookPack, Inc.

The authors and publisher have made every effort to ensure the accuracy of information contained in *Weekend Adventure Getaways: Monterey, Carmel, Big Sur, Santa Cruz*, but can accept no liability for any loss, injury, or inconvenience sustained by any traveler as a result of information or advice contained in this guide.

write to us
....

If in your travels you discover a spot that captures the spirit of California's Central Coast, or if you live in the region and have a favorite place to share, or if you just feel like expressing your views, write to us and we'll pass your note along to the author.

We can't guarantee that the author will add your personal find to the next edition, but if the writer does use the suggestion, we'll acknowledge you in the credits and send you a free copy of the new edition.

ULYSSES PRESS
P.O. Box 3440
Berkeley, CA 94703
E-mail: readermail@ulyssespress.com

table of contents
....

MAPS

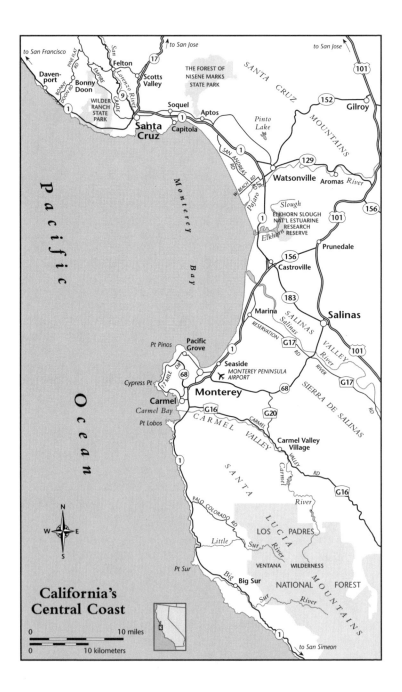

to San Francisco

Daven-
port
Bonny
Doon
WILDER
RANCH
STATE
PARK

Felton
Scotts
Valley
17

to San Jose

THE FOREST OF
NISENE MARKS
STATE PARK

SANTA

CRUZ

to San Jose

101

Soquel
Santa
Cruz
Capitola
Aptos

Pinto
Lake

152

MOUNTAINS

Gilroy

Monterey

Bay

SAN ANDREAS RD

1

W. BEACH RD

Pajaro

129

Watsonville
Aromas River

156

Slough
ELKHORN SLOUGH
NAT'L ESTUARINE
RESEARCH
RESERVE

101

Elkhorn

Prunedale

156

Castroville

183

Pacific
Ocean

Pt Pinos
Pacific
Grove

Cypress Pt

Marina

RESERVATION

1

Seaside
MONTEREY PENINSULA
AIRPORT

68

17 MILE DRIVE

SALINAS

Salinas

Salinas

G17

VALLEY

River

Salinas

101

RD

G17

Carmel

Carmel Bay

Pt Lobos

Monterey

68

G16

CARMEL

68

G20

CARMEL

SIERRA DE SALINAS

RD

VALLEY

Carmel Valley
Village

Carmel

VALLEY

RD

River

G16

1

SANTA

PALO COLORADO

RD

LUCIA

LOS PADRES

Little

Sur

River

VENTANA

WILDERNESS

NATIONAL FOREST

MOUNTAINS

Pt Sur

Big Sur

Big

Sur

River

1

to San Simeon

N
W E
S

California's
Central Coast

0   10 miles
0   10 kilometers

California's
Central Coast

$\int$ urfers, painters, winemakers, adventurers, authors, students, biologists, innkeepers, hermits and dilettantes have long been drawn to the coast of Monterey Bay and Big Sur like pelicans to a fishing boat. Even for travelers who are just passing through on Route 1, it's easy to see why. Start with the shoreline itself, a hundred-mile procession of soft, cream-colored sand beaches, scenic coastal shelves, wetlands teeming with birds and sea otters, and granite headlands from which, on a clear day, the views hint at infinity. Add gorges filled to overflowing with majestic redwood forests and broad, golden valleys where small farmers produce specialty crops like strawberries, artichokes, garlic, Brussels sprouts and premium varietal grapes. Set it all against a fortresslike backdrop of dark, steep mountains

that guard this magical empire from the world outside. Create more than two dozen state parks and beaches and you have a prescription for paradise (in a foggy sort of way).

Perhaps the greatest mystery about the Monterey Bay area is why everybody in California hasn't decided to move here. The total population of Santa Cruz and Monterey counties today is only one-fourth that of the city of Oakland. Certainly, there was a time when Californians had every reason to expect that this region was destined to become *the* "Bay Area." For nearly a century, under Spanish colonial, Mexican and United States rule, Monterey was the capital of California and one of the largest towns on the North American West Coast. Then the Gold Rush of 1849 shifted commerce north to the formerly small town of San Francisco and the capital to Sacramento, both stopovers on the journey to the gold fields of the Sierra foothills, and the past glories of Monterey were, at least briefly, forgotten.

Opposite: Lone Cypress.

After Monterey Bay became U.S. territory, would-be robber barons arrived to extract and sell its natural resources. Through the last half of the 19th century, fortunes were made by cutting down ancient redwood trees and by harpooning whales, whose oily blubber was the main source of fuel for heating and lighting American homes. When the largest remaining redwoods could only be found too deep in the rugged mountains to profitably haul out, and when petroleum and electricity came to provide cheaper alternatives to whale oil, the economy of the Monterey Bay area floundered briefly and was revived by another "inexhaustible" resource—sardines, which were then so plentiful that it's said people

Point Lobos, Big Sur.

could wade a few feet offshore and scoop up
handfuls of the tiny fish. Yet within the space of
a few decades, the last sardines had been caught,
canned and shipped off to become hors
d'oeuvres, leaving in their wake only abandoned
canneries and a famous novel by Nobel
Prize–winning local author John Steinbeck.
It was then that Santa Cruz, Monterey, Big Sur
and the other communities along the coast were
forced to acknowledge that only one facet of
their economy was truly unlimited: tourists.
Today, everything about the region is geared
toward preserving the natural beauty and
cultural uniqueness that entice pleasure travelers
to experience it for themselves.

Above all, Monterey Bay and Big Sur are for
active men and women. Although museums, art

galleries, gourmet restaurants and wonderful little inns abound, along with a handful of large-

scale sightseeing attractions like Santa Cruz's boardwalk and Monterey's world-famous aquarium, all these take a back seat to personal sports. Santa Cruz holds the richly deserved title of "Surf City USA." Pebble Beach *means* great golf, and its reputation spills over to a dozen other world-class courses around the bay. Scuba divers find limitless possibilities for exploring the undersea cliffs and kelp forests at the edges of the bay. Beaches and forest trails beckon hikers, mountain bikers and equestrians. The skies invite kiteboarders and hang gliders. Travelers whose idea of a good time is a full tank of gas, a clean windshield and the open road will discover a myriad of scenic routes and detours as they explore this one-of-a-kind microcosm, where you're more likely to catch sight of a sea lion colony or a whale than a typical American shopping mall.

Monterey Bay lies approximately 90 miles south of San Francisco and has a shoreline spanning 42 miles. It is bounded on the north by the redwood-clad Santa Cruz Mountains, 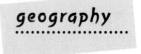 on the east by the agricultural Salinas Valley and the Gabilan Mountains, and on the south by the near-vertical wall of the Santa Lucia Mountains, so hard to penetrate that they blocked the coastal area known as Big Sur from settlement well into the 20th century.

All areas covered in this book are reached via Route 1, which is a multilane divided freeway from Santa Cruz to Monterey and an edgy two-lane highway south from there to Big Sur. Route 1 is also one of the most scenic routes for reaching Santa Cruz from the San Francisco Bay Area, though Route 9 over the Santa Cruz Mountains from Los Gatos offers strong competition in the scenery department. The fastest way from

Pacific Grove shoreline.

the Bay Area is via Route 17 from San Jose. Motorists coming from the south can either take Route 1 through Big Sur or come up Route 101, exiting at Salinas.

flora
....

The most obvious component of the forest surrounding Monterey Bay is the coast redwood, the world's tallest plant species. This tree, which grows only in the coastal fog belt from the Santa Lucia Mountains north to the California state line, can reach heights of up to 360 feet. Some redwoods are among the earth's oldest living things. One specimen cut down for lumber in 1933 was determined to be 2200 years old, though most ancient redwoods found in the region today average around 600 years old. For more than a century, redwoods were the preferred construction material in many parts of the United States, being both strong and easy to work as well as unusually resistant to termites and rot, so the large majority of old-growth trees were cut down before remaining stands were set aside in state and

Redwood tree.

federal parks; restrictions were imposed on the harvesting of the forest giants even on private land owned by forest products corporations. Today, a fascinating new phenomenon has appeared in some areas that were formerly clearcut: new seedlings nursed on the stumps of felled redwoods have grown to maturity, forming "fairy circles" of as many as a dozen tall trees in a tight cluster around a decaying stump.

But size isn't everything. Another tree at least as rare as the redwood is the Monterey cypress, a beautifully gnarled tree that originally grew in the highlands of the Monterey peninsula and in a few spots as far south as Big Sur. Most cypress trees have been started in nurseries and transplanted for landscaping purposes by homeowners, developers or municipalities. Only two native stands of Monterey cy-

OPPOSITE: Monterey Harbor.

press exist in the world, both in the mansion-and-golf-course community of Pebble Beach, which also has one of the only two stands of a related species, the pygmy Gowen cypress; the other stand is a few miles south at Point Lobos. The fossil record shows that cypresses like these were around even before the first dinosaurs walked the earth, making the tenuousness of their grip on survival all the more tragic.

An abundance of other trees, particularly pines, oaks and cottonwoods, grow near water in the forests around Monterey Bay. The one to be aware of is poison oak, which grows profusely in many parks and other hiking areas. Warning signs are often posted showing how to identify the leaves; however, poison oak is equally toxic even in the winter when it loses its leaves. To make matters worse, it can take many shapes—a tree, a bush, a ground-running shrub or a vinelike tree climber. The burning rash from contact with poison oak can usually be prevented by washing with soapy water immediately after a hike. By far the main source of poisoning, however, is petting a dog that has come in contact with the oak; the fur can retain the toxin for days. For this reason, dogs should be supervised

carefully while hiking, and most area parks and hiking trails have leash requirements.

One of the pleasures of Santa Cruz, Monterey and Carmel, as well as the wild meadows of nearby valleys, is the fact that almost any flowering plant imaginable thrives in the mild, moist microclimate around the bay. The result is fantastic gardens that fill neighborhoods with bright colors most of the year and are the subject of garden tours offered by many communities. Over the years, the distinction between garden flowers and wildflowers has blurred as birds and wind have spread seeds far and wide. Today, exotic flower species from Europe, Australia and Asia are sometimes found even in the deepest, hardest-to-reach redwood forests.

Growing conditions in the Monterey Bay area also make it an ideal place for experimental gardens and arboretums. Gardening enthusiasts can spend weeks touring them all. Commercial nurseries also often maintain large, parklike demonstration gardens that are open to the public, including one in Aptos that grows only bamboo—50 different species of it.

Last but not least, some parts of the bay are known for their underwater forests of kelp and sea palm. One of the several kelp species, giant kelp, grows to heights

Big Sur wildflower.

of more than 100 feet. These seaweed species root in the ocean floor and stand upright by growing hollow floats. Scuba divers find a special attraction in kelp forests, which provide shelter for a wide variety of fish, and surfers find the stuff an entangling nuisance. Landlubbers can view a three-story-high living kelp forest in the Monterey Bay Aquarium. Storms at sea commonly uproot kelp and cast it ashore in tangled piles called "wrack." Kelp is edible, and although it is rarely featured in area restaurants, kelp wrack is an important food source for shorebirds.

The most common large mammals in the region are black-tailed deer and mule deer, which may be encountered anywhere from the forests of Big Sur to the golf courses of Pebble Beach. Coyotes also roam

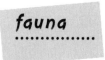

fauna

just about everywhere. Mountain lions and bobcats tend to avoid populated areas and, being nocturnal, are rarely sighted, though as more humans venture farther into the wilderness, especially in the Big Sur and Santa Lucia Mountains area, encounters with mountain lions are becoming more common.

Cormorants on Bird Island, Point Lobos.

Grizzly bears and elk, once native to the area, are no longer found here, though there have been occasional unconfirmed reports of black bears in the Ventana Wilderness.

Birders sometimes remark on the fact that any time during daylight hours, in any place, town or country, around Monterey Bay and Big Sur, the sound of bird calls is a constant presence. Sandpipers and godwits dash up and down the beaches just inches ahead of the surf. Terns and gulls swoop along the shoreline and hover above marinas, wharfs and old cannery piers. Brown pelicans and cormorants cluster in nesting colonies on offshore rock formations. Egrets, kingfishers and great blue herons hunt for frogs and fish in the wetlands of Elkhorn Slough. Kestrels, hawks, vultures and eagles glide over the hillsides that fringe the surrounding mountain ranges, and wild turkeys bound through the open meadows. Migrating ducks and geese congregate in the coastal lagoons. So profuse is the area's avian life that one wildlife refuge just 15 miles from downtown Monterey holds the Audubon Society record for the most bird species ever sighted in a single day anywhere in the United States.

But birds aren't the only beautiful creatures that fill the skies of Monterey Bay. The area is also where virtually all monarch butterflies that live west of the Continental Divide migrate to spend the winter. On sunny winter days, visitors to one of the butterfly sanctuaries in Santa Cruz or Pacific Grove will be rewarded with the sight of thousands of the bright-orange-and-black insects fluttering and tumbling through the air among the eucalyptus trees.

The greatest diversity of life in the region is found beneath the ocean's surface. Common fish range from the surf perch and rockfish that anglers reel in on municipal wharfs to the salmon, swordfish and huge tuna that run farther out toward the mouth of the bay. There are also 22 species of sharks, including the 20-foot great white shark of *Jaws* fame that, the California Department of Fish and Game assures us, does not live up to its fearsome reputation.

Squid dart through the water in such abundance that it's hard to find a restaurant in Monterey whose menu doesn't feature fresh calamari. Visitors who climb out on the rocks at the water's edge as low tide approaches may find anything from starfish, periwinkles, anemones and sea urchins to hermit crabs and red octopi.

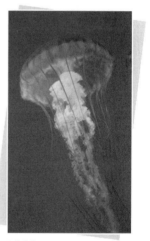

Sea otters, until recently a species poised on the brink of extinction, have made a remarkable recovery thanks to strict protective laws and are now commonly seen throughout the Monterey Bay and Big Sur region, often floating on their backs as they bob up and down on the waves using their stomachs as tables to dine on clams and shellfish. Harbor seals and California sea lions sprawl in close-packed groups on secluded beaches and off-

Jellyfish.

shore rocks in plain view of vista points by the side of Route 1. Dolphins glide beneath the surface of the bay and sometimes approach for a close-up look at human sea kayakers.

Most fascinating of all the region's marine mammals are the whales that can often be viewed from tour boats and sometimes seen from such shoreline vantages as Davenport and Point Lobos. Whale watching reaches its peak during the winter migration of gray whales, which travel down the coast from Alaska to the lagoons of Baja California, where the extremely saline

Sea otter.

water provides the extra buoyancy needed to make birthing easier. When the Baja lagoons were discovered by whalers from Monterey and San Francisco in the late 19th century, the West Coast gray whales were hunted to near-extinction within less than a decade; only in the 1980s did their population return to previous numbers. Today, at the peak of the migration gray whales travel past Monterey Bay at an average rate of more than 3000 a day. At other times of year, many other species of whales sometimes enter the bay with its extraordinarily deep water and rich food supply. A summer whale-watching jaunt can sometimes be rewarded with a look at a humpback, orca, sperm whale or even an 85- to 100-foot-long blue whale, the largest living animal on earth.

The Monterey Bay area has more than its share of endangered species—a fact that has proven instrumental in protecting so much of the coastline from development. Sea otters, gray whales and brown pelicans are among the formerly endangered species that have recovered from near-extinction. Some of the other creatures in the area that remain on the endangered species list today are less familiar: the snowy plover, the marbled murrelet, the tidewater gobie, Santa Cruz long-toed salamander, the great white shark, the legless lizard and the Smith's blue butterfly, as well as several species of bats.

geology

The origin of the mountain ranges that surround Monterey Bay is clear. They were formed as the land buckled from the agonizingly slow but inexorable shift of two tectonic plates—the Continental Plate, on which most of the United States rests, and the Pacific Plate, which lies beneath the ocean floor. The San Andreas Fault runs along the line where the two plates meet and is responsible for California's notorious earthquakes. The last major earthquake, which caused walls and freeways to collapse and killed or injured many residents in San Francisco in 1989, had its epicenter in The Forest of Nisene Marks just a few miles east of Santa Cruz, whose downtown area was all but demolished by the quake. Each such disaster is fresh evidence that the imperceptibly gradual process of mountain-building continues today.

More perplexing is the origin of Monterey Bay's most distinctive undersea feature, a canyon that splits the ocean floor to an average depth equal to the deepest part in the Grand Canyon—about a mile—and in some places, just a few miles offshore, reaches depths of 10,000 feet. Geologists once believed that the canyon was formed when the ocean floor off the coast was still above the water's surface, speculating that the river system that now flows into San Francisco Bay veered farther south in the distant past to cut a Grand Canyon–like gorge. More recently, oceanographers have concluded that the process is ongoing and much more complex, involving sediments that accumulate on the edge of the continental shelf and then crash into the deep ocean, causing sudden "turbidity currents" that erode the floor of the bay. Frequent underwater rockslides

Garrapata State Park, south of Carmel.

widen the canyon and accelerate the erosion process. The result is one of the deepest points in the Pacific Ocean so close to land, bringing big game fish and strange denizens of the deep sea close to shore. Modern technological advances such as mapping sonar and underwater video cameras (like the one monitored at the Monterey Bay Aquarium) have made this wonder of the world visible to human eyes for the first time.

when to go
....

Like most of the California coast, the area enjoys what's known as a Mediterranean climate (also found in parts of Australia, South Africa and Chile), meaning that winter weather is generally cool and rainy, though rarely below freezing, while summer tends to be dry and warm. This gross generalization is not as much help as one might think in actually predicting the kind of weather to expect during your visit. Though relatively small in area, Monterey Bay and Big Sur encompass not one but several "microclimates" in which the weather can vary so dramatically in the space of just a few miles that a short drive can make you feel as if you'd traveled to a completely different season.

Summer is peak tourist season, partly because, as popular family destinations, Santa Cruz and Monterey fill up when

Carmel Mission.

school lets out and partly because the ocean temperature rises in summer (though not high enough to leave your wet suit at home). The drawback is that July and August also get the most fog, and parts of Monterey Bay—especially around Moss Landing and Elkhorn Slough—are among the foggiest places in California. In fact, fog is the most serious road hazard along this part of Route 1, since it can blow in off the sea so suddenly that you barely have time to fine a good place to pull off the road. (It can also burn off just as quickly and be warm and sunny for the rest of the day.) Curiously, even when the east side of Monterey Bay and the highway from Point Lobos to Big Sur are socked in, the beach at Carmel is typically sunny and ten degrees warmer than other parts of the coast. As you travel inland through

Larkin House, Monterey.

the Salinas Valley or Carmel Valley, summer temperatures quickly become much hotter. This is also true of the surrounding mountains, though even when daytime temperatures climb into the 90s, they suddenly plunge into the 50s or 60s when the sun goes down.

Autumn is the nicest season to travel in this region. There is a lot of sunshine and little fog, and summerlike temperatures linger all the way through October. The summer tourist crowds fade away. Beach scenes become relaxed during the week, and you may even have a chance to enjoy a surfside picnic in solitude. You can pick out a restaurant on impulse and get in without reservations. All this changes on warm weekends, however, when it can sometimes seem as if everybody in the San Francisco Bay Area has decided to take a jaunt down Route 1 at the same time.

Although winter is known as the rainy season, it is more accurately characterized as wildly unpredictable. On the average, temperatures in midwinter are not really that much lower than in summer. It's just that changes in the weather tend to be extreme. A picture-perfect 72-degree day may set the stage for a ferocious three-day sea storm that sends walls of water crashing against the sea bluffs and buries beaches in soggy wracks of kelp. The mountains—especially the wild Santa Lucias south of Carmel Valley and east of Big Sur—can become extremely dangerous as floods wash out motorists, trapping the occasional fool-hardy motorist or hiker. The good news is that, while an occasional sprinkling of snow may whiten mountain ridges like powdered sugar for a morning before melting off, the coast and lowland valleys virtually never experience

snow or ice. The last recorded snowfall on the Monterey Peninsula was in 1962. The tourist trade does not slack off in winter as much as one might expect, either. After the Christmas shopping season, which some prosperous individuals consider an excellent excuse to visit Carmel-by-the-Sea, two quite different migrations—gray whales and monarch butterflies—bring waves of nature lovers to the area. Many charter-boat operators report that their busiest time of year is not the summer sportfishing season but the winter whale-watching season.

One of the best things about Monterey Bay's winters is that they're short. March comes in like a lamb, and flowers burst into bloom like Independence Day fireworks. Spring tends to be as sunny as fall, continuing through June before fog becomes the norm. Whether you're trekking across wild meadows or strolling among the parks and gardens of Santa Cruz, Carmel-by-the-Sea or historic Monterey, *Opposite: Monarch butterflies, Pacific Grove.*

if flowers make your heart sing then be prepared for a heavenly chorus.

packing & preparation

At the top of the list of things to take on any Monterey Bay trip is the sporting equipment you need for your choice among the many recreational opportunities there. This could mean gear as portable as a fishing tackle box, a bag of golf clubs or a backpack, tent and sleeping bag. It could mean getting your scuba tank filled or your parasail packed for a day of kiteboarding. Or it could involve the challenge of wrestling mountain bikes, a kayak or a surfboard onto your car's roof rack.

Besides sports gear, your car or RV can probably carry more than you will actually need. Many people tend to overpack because anticipation of a vacation trip can manifest itself in thoughts like, "What if we find a roadside stand selling fresh vegetables . . . .We might want the electric wok!" Packing light, a common adventure-travel mantra, may keep us from feeling silly when we look at all the extraneous stuff we brought along, but the fact remains—as road trippers we can usually find a spot somewhere, under a seat or in a corner of the trunk, for the wok and anything else we feel compelled to bring. The problem is, after a couple of days on the road and living out of our

View along the 17 Mile Drive.

vehicles in campgrounds or motels, all that carefully packed stuff starts to expand like an air bag, filling the whole car or motorhome with laundry, unfolded maps, mini-shampoo bottles, rolls of film and empty corn-chip bags, as well as all the other items we had to rummage through to find the things we wanted to pull out. At that point we realize that backpack travelers have it right: Pack light!

Biking along Monterey's waterfront.

The key consideration for visiting Monterey Bay and Big Sur at any time of year is to plan your clothing in layers—the more and thinner, the better. A foggy flannel-shirt-and-windbreaker morning can turn hot enough for a tank top in a matter of hours, then become windy enough to send your hat flying down the beach. If all the layers are color-coordinated, you can also pass for well-dressed at almost any restaurant in Monterey or Carmel. Although hiking boots with good ankle support are best for mountain hiking, if you plan on exploring rocky shores and tidepools, athletic shoes that stay flexible when squishy and dry quickly are a better footwear choice.

Speaking of appropriate attire, if you're planning on scuba diving, surfing or any other activity that involves immersing yourself in Monterey Bay, a wet suit is a must. In fact, wet suits were invented in Santa Cruz and are said to be responsible for the popularization of surfing there. In 1997, a warming El Niño in the Pacific Ocean raised the water temperature in Monterey Bay so much that for two months surfers could venture out wearing only bathing suits. They still talk about it wistfully today, though it hasn't happened since.

Travel information on Santa Cruz and the northern half of Monterey Bay can be found at the **Santa Cruz County Conference & Visitors Council**. ~ 1211 Ocean Street,

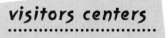

visitors centers
•••••••••••••••••••••••••••

Santa Cruz; 831-425-1234, 800-833-3494, fax 831-425-1260; www.santacruzca.org, e-mail comments@santacruzca.org. For the southern half of Monterey Bay, Monterey, Carmel and Big Sur, there's the **Monterey County Convention and Visitors' Bureau**. ~ 150 Olivier Street, Monterey; 831-649-1770, 888-221-1010, fax 831-648-5373; www.montereyinfo.org, e-mail info@mccvb.org.

Information on specific locales, with emphasis on member accommodations, restaurants and commercial attractions, is also available from chambers of commerce in most towns around the bay. They include the **Santa Cruz Chamber of Commerce** (611 Ocean Street, Santa Cruz; 831-457-3713), the **Capitola Chamber of Commerce** (716 Capitola Avenue, Capitola; 831475-6522), the **Aptos Chamber of Commerce** (7605 Old Dominion Court, Aptos; 831-688-1467, fax 831-688-6961), the **Moss Landing Chamber of Commerce** (8071 Moss Landing Road, Moss Landing; 831-633-4501), the **Marina Chamber of Commerce** (211 Hillcrest Avenue, Marina; 831-384-9155), the **Salinas Chamber of Commerce** (119 East Alisal Street, Salinas; 831-424-7611), the **Monterey Peninsula Chamber of Commerce** (380 Alvarado Street, Monterey; 831-648-5360), the **Pacific Grove Chamber of Commerce** (Forest Avenue at Central Avenue, Pacific Grove; 831-373-3304), the **Carmel Business Association** (Carmel; 831-624-2522) and the **Big Sur Chamber of Commerce** (831-667-2100).

For a lot of people, hiking is the main reason to visit Big Sur, where parks such as Andrew Molera State Park, Pfeiffer Big Sur State Park and Julia Pfeiffer Burns State Park offer fabulous trails of all lengths and difficulties.

hiking

Some Monterey Bay visitors may not even realize the many hiking possibilities. Trailheads are often not conspicuous. In fact, in some places locals have actually been known to take down signs so that hordes of outsiders won't "spoil" their favorite beaches and redwood groves. A few of the great hiking spots you'll find in this guide are Santa Cruz's Wilder Ranch State Park, The Forest of Nisene Marks State Park near Aptos, Elkhorn Slough near Moss Beach, Garland Ranch Regional

Park in Carmel Valley and Point Lobos State Reserve south of Carmel-by-the-Sea. All hikes in these areas are day trips. For a multiday backpacking trek, the best option is the Ventana Wilderness south of Carmel Valley and east of Big Sur. No permit is required at any of these places.

Hike with others. Even on one-mile walks to a nearby waterfall, find at least one other person to hike with you. If your plans call for hiking at least five hours away from human habitation, go with two other people, and if you're hiking into a wilderness area, your group should ideally be made up of at least four people, but no more than 12. That way, if someone is hurt, one person can stay with the injured party while two others go for help.

Before setting out on a hike, check the weather forecast. Tell someone where you're going and when you expect to be back. Take your cell phone. The reception can be surprisingly good in the mountains, particularly on high ridges or lakes, making search and rescue operations easier than ever before. Leave your number with the same person you leave your route plans with.

Rangers will tell you that even on a short hike each group member should pack water, water-purifying tablets, extra clothing, adhesive bandages or moleskin, sunglasses, a pocket knife, a whistle, any prescription medicines you may require, an extra pair of prescription glasses, an emergency shelter (such as bright-colored trash bags or lightweight plastic tarp) and waterproof matches or a fire starter. At least one person in the group should carry a complete first-aid kit, insect repellent, sunscreen, a flashlight with extra batteries and bulbs, toilet paper, a latrine shovel or baggies for solid waste, a watch, pens and paper, and an emergency kit containing a topographical map and compass, a metal mirror, 20 to 25 feet of nylon rope, and an emergency signaling device. However, hikers are also routinely advised that their gear should not exceed one-third of their body weight, which suggests that you may want to take the official recommended list with a grain of salt and consider what's really important. Otherwise, you may find yourself three miles up the trail, wondering why bears don't have to carry all this stuff.

Most of the campgrounds in this guide are operated by state and local parks. Very few of them offer motorhome utility hookups—electricity, water or sewer. A few have dumping stations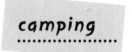

camping

where RVs can empty their sewage holding tanks on the way out. Some campgrounds have limits on the length of motorhomes or trailers they can accommodate. Most state park campgrounds take reservations, and it's best to plan your stops ahead and make reservations, especially during the summer months and on weekends. Camping reservations at California state parks can be made by contacting 800-444-7275, www.reserveamerica.com. In a few instances where state park campgrounds in the area are designed to accommodate tenters only, or perhaps small RVs, this guide includes an outstanding private RV park option.

Motorhomers can rest assured that a number of other private RV parks are available on the east side of Monterey Bay and in Big Sur. There is almost no camping of any kind on the Monterey Peninsula itself.

lodging & dining

Monterey and Carmel are justly renowned for their fine restaurants, and just about every community covered in this guide boasts exceptional dining in all price ranges. The price categories are relative and based on the lowest full-meal price on the menu: *budget*—$9 or less; *moderate*—$9 to $18; *deluxe*—$18 to $25; and *ultra-deluxe*—more than $25. In most lower-priced restaurants, the entrée price and tip are all you need to consider. In ultra-deluxe places, there are $15 appetizers, carafes of unbelievably good central California wines and accordingly large tips, so it's best to savor these dining experiences and realize that "more than $25" per person might mean $300 for you and a date. Most likely a good deal—ask your date.

Beachside dining in Santa Cruz.

The situation with lodging rates can be somewhat more restrictive, since inns and resorts that don't charge a small fortune are few and far between in Monterey, Pebble Beach and Carmel. There are a scattering of moderate-priced motels, of course, but they book up fast. Other areas, especially Santa Cruz, have a wide range of accommodations in terms of both price and quality. Price ranges in this guide are based on the high-season (summer) rate for a double. Room rates may be significantly lower in spring or fall, and some places have large suites with more amenities such as fireplaces, jacuzzis or balconies at much higher rates. Rate structures may change frequently. As this edition goes to press, the relative room rate categories are: *budget*—less than $60 a night for two people; *moderate*—$60 to $120 a night; *deluxe*—$120 to $175 a night; and *ultra-deluxe*—more than $175 a night (in a few instances, *much* more. A couple of resorts included in this guide have suites that rent for as close to $1000 a night).

Opposite: Pfeiffer Big Sur Beach.

kids
....

Monterey Bay is among the most family-friendly places in California. From the Santa Cruz Boardwalk to the Monterey Bay Aquarium, many of the area's best sightseeing attractions were designed with kids in mind. Better yet, the abundance of wildlife can

make a family visit to the area not only fun but . . . shhhhh . . . educational. Supervise children closely, however, around attractive hazards such as sea cliffs, large rocks and beaches, especially those where an absence of swimmers suggests the possibility of dangerous undertows or surprise waves.

If you're planning to hike, start with a short, easy trail and learn your children's present walking rates. It takes longer—sometimes *much* longer—to hike the same distance with children. They have shorter strides. They often tend to expend a lot of energy quickly and run short of stamina, and they can distract themselves and you with the

Santa Cruz Boardwalk.

most interesting observations of nature. Bring plenty of sunscreen, insect repellent and snacks.

With the exception of a handful of fancy B&Bs and one or two exclusive resorts, the lodgings listed in this guide welcome children.

pets
....

Dogs make great companions on a camping trip but can pose a problem if you plan to sleep indoors. More so than in most other areas of California, lodgings—not only gingerbready B&Bs and upscale resorts but also run-of-the-mill motels and motor inns—will not accommodate dogs. The best solution to this problem is to contact the local convention and visitors bureau or chamber of commerce, which maintains a complete (and surprisingly short) list of lodgings that accept pets. Anywhere you stay with a dog, you can expect to pay an extra fee—typically a dollar or two at campgrounds and around $10 at motels.

Both Santa Cruz and Monterey counties have leash laws that apply not only in town but also in rural areas. Most California state parks in this region allow dogs on hiking trails but also require them to be on a leash not longer than seven feet. Dogs are not always allowed on beaches—look for posted signs. In protected wildlife areas such as Elkhorn Slough, dogs are *canis non gratis*. Leash laws do not apply in the Ventana Wilderness.

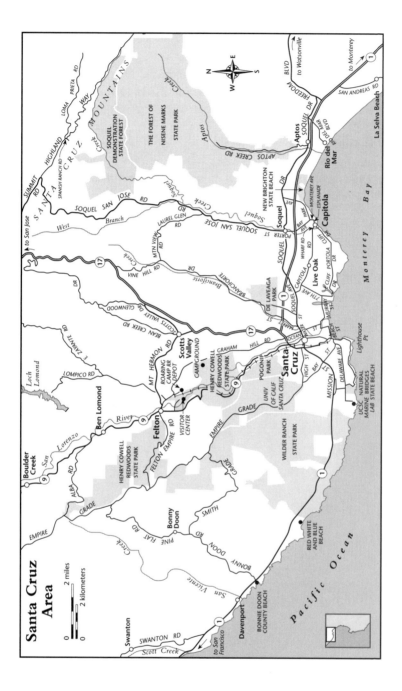

Santa Cruz Area

0 ___ 2 miles
0 ___ 2 kilometers

2

Santa Cruz

eparated from Silicon Valley by a redwood-clad, often foggy mountain range, Santa Cruz is a world apart from the hectic mainstream just half an hour's drive away. Weekend escapees and long-term refugees from Bay Area cities have been flocking here since the 1870s for the spectacular mix of sandy beaches and sea cliffs that rim the north side of Monterey Bay. Venerable old-time attractions such as the boardwalk amusement park and the excursion train from the beach to the redwoods continue to please generations of tourists.

The artistic community has embraced Santa Cruz for as long as tourism has and as the number and quality of galleries grows apace with the impressive array of theater venues, its reputation continues to rise. The town's

cultural life got a big boost in 1965 with the arrival of the University of California at Santa Cruz, and today college students account for 20 percent of Santa Cruz's total population of 51,000. Somehow the laidback quality of life has endured in spite of the influx of Silicon Valley money that has made the cost of living in Santa Cruz County the third-highest in the country.

Another aspect of the local lifestyle becomes apparent on first sight of the ocean. Santa Cruz *is* "Surf City USA." The nickname identifies everything from a local chapel to a coffee company and a golf tournament, not to mention the Surf City Sirens women's rugby team. In fact, several years ago when the Southern California community of Huntington Beach brought a lawsuit to establish its exclusive right to the words "Surf City" (from the 1963 Jan and Dean song, co-authored by Beach Boy Brian Wilson, which was the first surfing record ever to hit number one on the charts), the court rejected the claim, declaring that the moniker rightly belonged to Santa Cruz.

Besides surfing, Santa Cruz offers a full range of other activities, including bicycling, skating, kayaking, kiteboarding and golfing (at one of the best, though not best-known, courses in the Monterey Bay area). Wild nature, too, surrounds Santa Cruz on all sides. This is one place where you might see whales, sea otters, starfish, deer, butterflies and a partridge in an ancient redwood tree—all in the same day.

sightseeing

Three- and four-story California Revival buildings—part Mediterranean, part gold camp—line **Mission Street** and **Pacific Avenue**, downtown Santa Cruz's main drags. The district crumbled under the impact of the Loma Prieta earthquake in October 1989 and was rebuilt in historical styles. During re-

construction, the city closed two lanes of the four-lane avenues and converted them into wide sidewalks lined with shade trees, creating the ambience of a pedestrian promenade without actually excluding cars. The facelift transformed Santa Cruz from hippie beach town to upscale weekend getaway almost overnight. Today downtown Santa Cruz is home to art galleries, high-end craft studios, wonderful bookstores and fashionable restaurants. ~ To get downtown, take the River Street exit from Route 1, at the junction with Route 9 from Redwood City, and one exit east of the intersection with Route 17 from

Pacific Avenue, downtown Santa Cruz.

Museum of Art and History at the McPherson Center.

San Jose. There are parking lots on Front Street, one block east of Pacific.

On Front Street, the **Museum of Art and History at the McPherson Center** presents changing displays of historical artifacts and photographs from Santa Cruz's early days, as well as traveling exhibits and works from its permanent collection of post–World War II regional art. The museum's history library, containing thousands of books, vintage photos and documents, is open to the public Tuesday through Thursday afternoons. Adjacent to the main museum building, the historic Octagon Building houses the **Museum Store**, where you'll find art, jewelry and educational toys as well as books on art and regional history. McPherson Center also presents evening lectures, films, docent-led gallery tours, family programs and workshops throughout the year. Closed Mondays. Admission; kids free. ~ 705 Front Street; 831-429-1964; www.santacruz mah.org, e-mail admin@santacruzmah.org.

Santa Cruz got its start in 1791 as a Spanish mission compound on the bank of the San Lorenzo River. Two years later the mission was moved brick by brick to a new hilltop location beyond the reach of the flood-prone river, where it commanded a sweeping view of the growing town below—until it was toppled by an earthquake in 1857. A half-size model of **Mission La Exaltación de la Santa Cruz** now stands across

from the church that occupies the original mission site and dwarfs the reconstruction. Closed Mondays. ~ 126 High Street; 831-426-5686.

More interesting is the 1822 adobe house at **Santa Cruz Mission Adobe State Historic Park**. One of the last remaining adobe structures in Santa Cruz, it is the oldest building in Santa Cruz County. Indians originally built it as a place to live while they worked at the mission. It housed up to 17 families and survived the destruction of the mission itself. Later the Indians sold it to a group of "Californios," or local Mexicans who stayed after California became U.S. territory in 1846. It was eventually sold again to an Irish family. The seven remaining rooms of the old adobe house are furnished and decorated in a sequence of historical styles reflecting the heritage of its various owners, including many artifacts that were excavated at the site. Also in the park is a scale model of the whole mission compound as it appeared at the time the adobe house was built. Closed Mondays through Wednesdays. ~ 144 School Street near Mission Plaza; 831-425-5849, fax 831-429-6748.

Continue south from downtown on Pacific Avenue to reach the waterfront near **Santa Cruz Municipal Pier**. Bait shops, boat-trip operators and fishmonger stalls share the half-mile-long wharf with optimistic anglers. Stroll out to the end for a new perspective on **Santa Cruz Beach**, the most popular and crowded of the three major beaches that span the Santa Cruz coastline. Viewed from the pier, the luxuriantly sandy beach languishes against a backdrop of classic beach-town Americana—motels by the day or week, T-shirt shops, snack bars, party-all-night clubs. In contrast to the city's newly spiffed-up downtown, many structures near the beach date back to the 1920s, creating the kind of cheerful nostalgia you'd expect if Norman Rockwell painted a Spring Break scene.

The best part of this beach, the **Santa Cruz Boardwalk** has been the town's pride and joy ever since it was built in 1907. Today it's a National Historic Landmark. Of the 34 rides and attractions, the showpiece is the Giant Dipper, a wooden rollercoaster constructed in 1924 and still considered by the American Coaster Enthusiasts Association to be one of the world's best. Nearby are a 1911 Charles Looff carousel, with more than 70 hand-carved wooden horses set around a 19th-

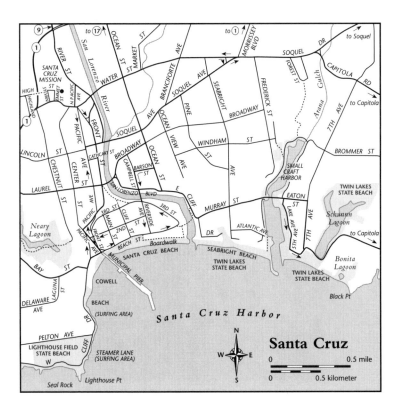

century pipe organ, and a Ferris wheel that gently lifts passengers high above boardwalk, beach and bay. Other attractions run the gamut from a bowling alley and a miniature golf course, the formerly fashionable Cocoanut Grove Ballroom (now used mainly for private functions) and an electronic arcade featuring laser tag, a virtual rollercoaster and a collection of vintage video games such as Pac-Man and Space Invaders. Admission to the boardwalk is free. There's an $8 parking fee and a charge for ride tickets. ~ 400 Beach Street; 831-423-5590; www.beachboardwalk.com.

Santa Cruz Boardwalk.

Whether you drive, stroll, bike or skim on a scooter along the two-and-a-half-mile rim of sea bluffs that run west from Santa Cruz Beach to Natural Bridges State Beach, the scenery will invite your soul to soar like a seagull. A block west of the municipal pier, Beach Street turns south along **Cowell Beach**, a mecca for novice surfers, and becomes **West Beach Drive**, a level shore-hugging road alongside a paved pedestrian, bicycle and skate pathway. The first segment of the drive, out to Lighthouse Point, used to be known as Millionaire's Row

View of the Santa Cruz Boardwalk from the Municipal Pier.

in the early 1900s, when each block was a private estate. The properties were later subdivided, and some of the mansions, such as the Darling House, were converted to bed-and-breakfast inns.

From Lighthouse Point, atmospheric conditions permitting, you can see the full 40-mile sweep of Monterey Bay. A broad expanse of lawn and evergreens, set aside as part of **Lighthouse Point State Beach**, keeps city noise at bay as onlookers line the metal railing along the point to watch surfers brave the waves of **Steamer Lane**, reputed to be the most challenging point break on the West Coast. On the other side of the point, California sea lions bark, jostle and bask in the sun a hundred yards offshore on **Seal Rock**.

A lighthouse has stood on **Lighthouse Point** since 1867; when the original one was demolished in the late 1940s, the Coast Guard erected a no-frills automatic beacon to take its place. When Mark Abbott, the son of renowned photographers and civic leaders Chuck and Esther Abbott, died while surfing Steamer Lane in the 1960s, his parents erected the present brick lighthouse with white Greek Revival–style trim as a memorial to him.

In 1986 Lighthouse Point's lighthouse was expanded to house the **Santa Cruz Surfing Museum**, where exhibits trace the sport's development from the massive 100-pound, 15-foot-

Santa Cruz Surfing Museum.

long boards made from redwood planks in the 1930s to the sleek, high-tech boards used today, and even a shark-bitten board. There's one of the first wet suits that enabled surfers from Southern California and Hawaii to challenge the much colder waters off Santa Cruz without turning blue, as well as a collection of historic photographs immortalizing the town's most prominent beach bums. Closed Tuesdays (and Wednesdays in winter). ~ West Cliff Drive at Lighthouse Point; 831-420-6289; www.santacruzmuseums.org/surfin.html, e-mail staff@santacruzmuseums.org.

Nearby, a larger-than-life **surfer statue** often bedecked with fresh flower wreaths depicts the late Wes Reed, known locally as the "Mayor of Cowell Beach." The last of the original Depression-era California surfers, Reed rode the waves around Santa Cruz for more than 60 years before retiring from the sport at age 81. He passed away six years later in 1999.

Natural Bridges State Park.

As West Cliff Drive continues its winding way above the sea, inconspicuous trails descend from vista points down to hidden coves, sea caves, arches and pocket beaches. At its west end, the coast route brings you to 65-acre **Natural Bridges State Beach**, named for the three connected arches that were formed from a sandstone cliff by water erosion. Only the middle bridge remains intact; the outermost, once a favorite picnic spot and wedding site for early-day Santa Cruz residents, collapsed around 1900, and the inner one fell during a 1980 storm. The small, crescent-shaped beach is a favorite windsurfing spot in summer. Tidepools near the west end offer a chance to see starfish, sea anemones and crabs in their natural habitat. Facilities include picnic areas, restrooms and a visitors center with a bookstore. No dogs allowed. Day-use fee. ~ West Cliff Drive; 831-423-4609; e-mail naturalbridges@ juno.com.

Seymour Marine Discovery Center.

Delaware Avenue marks the northern boundary of Natural Bridges State Beach. Follow this avenue to the end to reach the **Seymour Marine Discovery Center** at Long Marine Lab. The most obvious wonder of the deep to be seen at this research and education facility of the University of California at Santa Cruz is a complete skeleton of an 87-foot blue whale, the earth's largest living creature. There are also touch tanks and interpretive exhibits designed for all school grade levels, including one that shows what sea life was like millions of years ago, but what sets the center apart from other aquariums and natural-history museums in the Monterey Bay area is the opportunity to watch scientists at work in an actual marine biology laboratory. Closed Mondays. Admission. ~ 100 Shaffer Road; 831-459-3800; seymourcenter.ucsc.edu.

From the western edge of Santa Cruz, a scenic 20-mile drive can show you a cross-section of the shoreline, fields, hills and

• •

King of the Butterflies

During the winter months, 10,000 to as many as 150,000 orange-and-black monarch butterflies converge on the nature preserve at Natural Bridges State Beach. All North American monarchs that spend the summer west of the Continental Divide migrate to small eucalyptus groves around Santa Cruz and other central California locales such as Pacific Grove and Pismo Beach. (Those from the eastern U.S. migrate to Cuba or Mexico.) Experts have been unable to agree on why the monarchs migrate while most other butterflies do not—and that's just one of the mysteries that surround these strange, fragile little beings.

Monarchs spread across the U.S. and Canada during the warm months, laying their eggs on milkweed, the only plants their larvae eat. The milkweed contains a chemical that makes both larvae and adult butterflies poisonous to birds. Monarchs born at that time of year live between two and three months, during which they breed and lay eggs, while those that mature close to migration time live for eight months, breeding only near the end of their stay in California and waiting to lay their eggs until they begin their journey inland. The butterflies that arrive in California in the fall are three generations removed from those that left the previous spring, yet they somehow find their way back to the same small groves that their ancestors left. Making this genetic enigma even more perplexing is the fact that identical monarch butterflies living in the tropics of Central America have no migratory instinct and, like most nonmigratory butterflies, have a life span of only about three weeks.

To learn more about monarchs, take one of the weekend guided tours offered from October to late February at Natural Bridges State Beach. Reservations are unnecessary. For scheduled times, call 831-423-4609.

• •

forest that surrounds the town. Start by heading north on Natural Bridges Road from the beach or Shaffer Road from the marine discovery center to join Route 1 northbound. In a little more than a mile you'll come to **Wilder Ranch State Park**, a historic dairy farm that operates as an open-air museum. Four generations of the Wilder family lived on the ranch from the 1880s to the 1970s. Their 1897 Victorian-style farmhouse shares its lawn and gardens with an 1850 farmhouse and an adobe house from old Mexican times, when El Rancho del Matadero, as the ranch was then known, was the largest agricultural estate in the Santa Cruz region. The houses, a blacksmith shop and other ranch buildings are open for self-guided tours, and volunteers present living-history demonstrations on weekends. Dairy cows and other farm animals live at the ranch. Five hundred acres of fields are under cultivation and produce more than ten percent of the Brussels sprouts sold in the U.S. To Santa Cruz locals, the best part of Wilder Ranch is its backcountry. With the acquisition of adjoining Gray Whale Ranch, the park sprawls across 7000 acres from the seashore to elevations of up to 1000 feet. Mountain bikers, hikers and equestrians love the 35 miles of trails that meander throughout the park's wild areas. No dogs allowed. Day-use fee. ~ 1401 Old Coast Road; 831-423-9703.

Beyond Wilder Ranch, the coastline boasts a number of secluded beaches, several of them clothing-optional and very popular. Watch for the American flag-colored mailbox that marks the turnoff to the privately owned **Red, White and Blue Beach**, a counterculture institution dating back to the '60s that is now frequented by baby boomers in RVs and nude families. No dogs, fires or cameras. Day-use fee, $10 per person. ~ Scaroni Road; phone/fax 831-423-6332.

Three miles farther up Route 1, across the highway from the Bonnie Doon Road intersection, **Bonny Doon County Beach** is an equally popu-
lar, less developed and free nude beach. Protected by a horseshoe of rugged cliffs, it has no security or facilities. That means no restrooms, outhouses or even large bushes for privacy. Strong currents make swimming dangerous. On the plus side, the atmosphere is the most re-

laxed and friendly of any beach in the area, and many patrons seem to be regulars who are on a first-name basis. ~ To get

there, leave your vehicle in the parking turnout along Route 1 and hike over the railroad tracks to the beach.

Continue your scenic drive by turning right (away from the ocean) on Bonny Doon Road. The turnoff is eight miles north of Santa Cruz and one mile south of the historic former whaling village of **Davenport**. The road winds up into the hills and through the forest community of **Bonny Doon**, its luxury homes so widely scattered among the pines and redwoods that it hardly seems to qualify as a "village." You'll pass the **Bonny Doon Vineyard**, one of some two dozen wineries and vineyards that surround Santa Cruz, open daily for tastings of its Rhone and Italian varietal wines. ~ 10 Pine Flat Road ad Bonny Doon Road; 831-425-4518; www.bonnydoonvineyard.com.

In the village, Bonny Doon Road becomes Pine Flat Road. Turn right where it intersects **Empire Grade** and you're in for a short, wild ride back to Santa Cruz. The winding road with rollercoaster hills descends through lush redwood forest, skirt-

ing the edge of Henry Cowell Redwoods State Park's Fall Creek Unit and continuing into the surprisingly wild backcountry of the **University of California at Santa Cruz** campus. If you stay on Empire Grade, it will take you back into town on High Street and return you to Route 1 at the point where it becomes a four-lane freeway. To see more of the university campus,

Merrill College, University of California at Santa Cruz.

turn left from Empire Grade at the west entrance gate. The main road through the campus changes names each time it changes directions, from Heller Drive to McLaughlin Drive, then—as it leaves the area of academic and residential buildings to continue through open rural country—to Glenn Coolidge Drive and finally Dickens Drive, before exiting the campus and becoming Bay Street. The university's buildings are internationally renowned for their architectural harmonization with the surrounding natural landscape. The

OPPOSITE: University of California at Santa Cruz.

stone ruins and sunbleached buildings near the south entrance at Dickens Drive and High Street are remains of the old Cowell Ranch, whose former owner endowed the University of California with the land UCSC now occupies. ~ 831-459-2190.

The university's main visitors attraction, the **UCSC Arboretum** is located along Empire Grade midway between the west and main entrance gates. The arboretum got its start

in 1964 with a gift from Australia of 90 different species of eucalyptus trees. It now has the largest collection of Australian plants and trees outside that country, as well as extensive collections of unusual plants from New Zealand and South Africa. Also awaiting visitors' discovery along the maze of trails that crisscross the arboretum are the world's largest assortment of conifer trees and shrubs, collections of cacti and native flowering plants of California, and an aroma garden redolent with mint, thyme, oregano, lavender and other fragrant herbs. ~ 1156 High Street; 831-427-2998; www2.ucsc.edu/arboretum/gardens.html.

Azalea.

Adjacent to the arboretum, the **UCSC Center for Agroecology & Sustainable Food Systems** has a pedestrian trail and bike path beside the fields as well as a gatehouse where agricultural and gardening workshops and plant sales are held on weekends from January to late November. A required one-day parking permit can be purchased for $5 at the main entrance information kiosk. ~ Coolidge Drive; 831-459-4140; www.ucsc.edu/casfs.

Can't get enough of the wild lands on the fringe of Santa Cruz? Then check out **Pogonip Open Space Preserve** and **Henry Cowell Redwoods State Park**, which flank Route 9 (River Street) along the eastern boundary of the UCSC campus. For more information on these areas, see "Hiking" in this chapter.

While most of Santa Cruz's "must-see" sightseeing highlights are located west of the San Lorenzo River, which bisects the town, there are more beaches east of the river. From the boardwalk area, take Riverside Avenue over the bridge and turn right on East Cliff Drive. **Seabright Beach** (also known as Castle Beach) lies between the river and the Santa Cruz Small Craft Harbor. Sheltered by sea cliffs, the beach is sandy and scenic but less crowded than others in Santa Cruz because the street layout makes it harder to get to. Facilities include restrooms and fire rings; in summer there's a lifeguard on duty. ~ East Cliff Drive at Seabright Avenue; 831-429-2850.

Just across the road from Seabright Beach, the small **Santa Cruz Museum of Natural History** has a life-size concrete statue of a gray whale in front. Inside are exhibits on local flora and fauna, a tidepool touch tank, a mural and artifacts recalling the way of life of the Ohlone Indians who once lived along this part of the coast, and fossils such as a mastodon skull. ~ 1305 East Cliff Drive; 831-420-6115; www.santacruz museums.org/exhibits.html.

WHATEVER FLOATS YOUR BOAT

One of Santa Cruz's most offbeat sporting traditions, the **Wednesday Night Sailboat Races** take place every week from April through October. The finish line is at the Santa Cruz Harbor's Crow's Nest Restaurant, and everyone's a winner. Would-be sailors can sign onto boat crews by showing up at the small craft harbor before 5:30 p.m. with a six-pack in hand (to assure the boat owners that you won't drink up all *their* beer).

Santa Cruz Museum of Natural History.

● ●

Historic Train Rides

Even before a network of narrow-gauge railroads was established to haul giant redwood logs out of the mountains in the1880s, the first railroad in the area began carrying tourists between Santa Cruz Beach and the redwood forests in 1875. Today, **Roaring Camp Railroads** operates diesel-powered trains with enclosed

coaches on the same route between the Santa Cruz Beach Boardwalk and the old lumbering center of Roaring Camp (now part of the village of Felton) through Henry Cowell Redwoods State Park, a three-hour roundtrip. The Beach Train runs twice daily in summer and weekends only from mid-May to mid-June and September through November, with evening Holiday Lights Trains on December weekend nights. The railroad company also operates narrow-gauge steam engines from Roaring Camp, pulling open passenger cars through redwood groves to the summit of Bear Mountain, a 75-minute roundtrip. The steam trains run four or five times daily from mid-June through August, once a day on weekdays and three times a day on Saturdays and Sundays in spring and fall, and weekends only from January through March. Fares are surprisingly reasonable, and reservations are essential. ~ P.O. Box G-1, Felton, CA 95018; 831-335-4484, fax 831-335-3509; www.roaringcamp.com, e-mail depot@roaringcamp.com.

● ●

East Cliff Drive is not continuous; it stops at the small craft harbor and resumes on the other side. To get across, take Seabright Drive north to Murray Street, which bridges the harbor, and then follow Lake Avenue south to rejoin East Cliff Drive at **Twin Lakes State Beach**. With the warmest stretch of sunlit sand in the area, this small beach bounded by rocks and waterfront residences is preferred by locals for family picnicking and kite flying. The 94-acre park also encompasses Schwann Lagoon, a wetland habitat for gulls, ducks, geese, kingfishers and various amphibians. The lagoon was one of the original "twin lakes"; the other, Woods Lagoon, was dredged to form the small craft harbor. ~ East Cliff Drive at 7th Avenue; 831-429-2850.

East Cliff Drive curves around to become Portola Drive, which continues through residential areas and returns to the shoreline at Capitola (see Chapter 3).

outdoor adventures

HIKING

All distances for hiking trails are one-way unless otherwise noted.

At Natural Bridges State Beach, the one-mile **Moore Creek Trail** leads through scrub meadows teeming with birds and down to the creek's wetlands before linking with the **Monarch Trail**, a half-mile nature path and boardwalk through the park's monarch butterfly nature preserve. As many as 150,000 butterflies winter here from October to late February, though their numbers—here as well as at other groves along the central California coast—vary widely from year to year. Most experts believe that the same "families" of monarchs return to the same locations every winter and that the populations vary because of mishaps thousands of miles away, such as storms

Wilder Ranch State Park.

during migration or the destruction by real estate developers of wild milkweed plants where the butterflies lay their eggs. (No dogs allowed.)

Of the 35 miles of trails at Wilder Ranch State Park, the best is the **Old Cove Landing Trail**, which starts from the east side of the headquarters parking lot. The three-mile trail is level and easy, though rocky. It meanders among scrub meadows, wetlands and fields of Brussels sprouts, reaching the seashore at a point overlooking an estuary at Wilder Beach, where Wilder Creek flows into the sea. The beach itself is closed to the public as a key habitat for endangered snowy plovers. From there, the trail turns west and hugs the rim of sea cliffs above the bay. Below the cliffs, pocket beaches and rock shelves look enticing but most are hard for humans to reach—which may explain the abundance of cormorants and other sea birds, as well as seals and otters, there. The most accessible is Fern Grotto Beach, named for the cave toward its west end where a year-round trickle of spring water sustains a mini-jungle of coastal ferns. The "official" end of the trail, where most hikers start back, is at a rocky point beyond the Fern Grotto Beach turnoff, though another branch, the Ohlone Bluffs Trail, continues for several more miles along the shoreline.

> If you have time for only one back-country hike in the Santa Cruz area, make it Wilder Ranch State Park's **Old Cove Landing Trail**, which combines sea cliffs, pocket beaches, fern grottoes, sea lions and Brussels sprouts for a fascinating coastline experience.

There are many more miles of trails in the backcountry that comprise most of Wilder Ranch State Park. All trails on the north side of Route 1 are shared by mountain bikers and equestrians, making them less appealing for some hikers. Some of these trails are described in the "Biking" section below.

Another old ranch turned natural area on Santa Cruz's outskirts, **Pogonip Open Space Preserve** has eight miles of trails, most of them for hikers only. The 640-acre undeveloped park was donated to the city of Santa Cruz by heirs of cement and timber tycoon Henry Cowell, who also endowed California with its adjoining state park and the University of California with the land for its Santa Cruz campus. In 1912 the land that is now Pogonip became the Casa del Rey Club and Golf Links. It went bankrupt in the Great Depression, and its clubhouse was reopened as the Pogonip Social and Polo Club, which raised eyebrows as one of the few polo grounds in America open to women's teams. Today the old clubhouse is fenced off awaiting restoration, the former polo grounds and golf course have gone back to the wild as meadows of tall grass, and a new generation of redwoods surrounds the park's three ancient ones. Blacktail deer and coyotes are sometimes seen, and a few hikers have spotted bobcats or mountain lions. There is an information kiosk with a trail map at the park entrance on Golf Club

Drive (limited on-street parking east of the railroad tracks) and another at the Glenn Coolidge Drive trailhead on the UCSC campus (day parking permit required). The easy two-mile **Pogonip Creek Nature Trail** starts at the Golf Club Drive entrance and leads past second-growth redwood stands, mixed woodlands, old orchards and wildflower meadows. Several other well-marked trails intersect the nature trail. A longer, three-mile loop can be made by turning left at the first trail intersection and following the relatively steep **Lookout Trail** with its outstanding view of Santa Cruz, then taking the **Spring**

Trail for a gentle walk through forests of redwood, maple and eucalyptus, and continuing through the woods on the Brayshaw Trail, which returns you to Golf Club Drive at the park ranger station. There are no restrooms, drinking water or phones. Dogs on leash are allowed, though owners are cautioned that they

••••••••••••••••••••••••••••

GO CLIMB A ROCK

Most Santa Cruz rock-climbing enthusiasts—and there are a lot of
them—head for cliffs inland from the
Monterey Bay area in areas like Castle Rock State Park and Pinnacles National Monument. So how do they
train between expeditions? Indoors,
that's how! **Pacific Edge Climbing
Gym** is one of the world's largest ar-
tificial climbing faces, 50 feet tall
with 13,000 square feet of state-of-
the-art climbing terrain including
caves, cracks and boulders. Instruc-
tional classes are offered for ages 6
through adult, of all skill levels. Both
memberships and one- or five-day
passes are available. ~ 104 Bronson
Street #12; 831-454-9254; www.pa
cificedgeclimbinggym.com.

••••••••••••••••••••••••••••

are more likely to contract a poison
oak rash from their dogs' fur than
from direct contact with the noxious
shrub, which is common in the park.
~ 333 Golf Club Drive; 831-420-5270;
www.santacruzparksandrec.com/
parks.pogo.html.

Adjoining Pogonip's northern
boundary, the 4000-acre **Henry
Cowell Redwoods State Park** has 18
miles of trails through ancient redwood groves, across sun-drenched hillsides and wildflower meadows; some
are multi-use trails for hikers, bikers,
equestrians and dog-walkers, while
others are reserved for hikers only. By
far the most used route in the park,
the .8-mile **Redwood Grove Nature
Trail**—an easy loop from the park's
nature center on Graham Hill Road—leads past some of the
park's largest redwoods, including one that stands almost 300
feet tall and 17 feet in diameter. From the same starting point,
Pipeline Road—a paved access road that follows the San Lo-

renzo River—is shared by hikers,
bikers and dogs (on leash), with
a horse trail paralleling it. After
about a mile, the road climbs
away from the river through fir,
oak and madrone forest to an ob-
servation deck and picnic area
with drinking water. Here, bikes
and horses are diverted onto the
Rincon Fire Road, while dogs
and their owners must turn back
the way they came. Hikers may want to continue on the 2.5-
mile loop formed by the **Ridge Fire Road**, descending to the

park campground, and the **Eagle Creek Trail**, returning to the
redwood groves and, eventually, to Pipeline Road for the last
leg of the walk back. Day-use fee, $5. ~ Graham Hill Road;
831-335-4598, fax 831-335-3156; www.mountainparks.org.

BIKING

Santa Cruz is one of the most bicycle-friendly cities
around, thanks in large part to pedal-powered UCSC
students. Local government has been enthusiastic in its com-
pliance with the California Bicycle Transportation Act. Any
part of town is easy to reach on "Class II" bike routes—wide,
striped cyclists' lanes on street or highway shoulders. Along
the Santa Cruz shore, the best "Class I" bike routes—paved
pathways apart from the road and wide enough to pass pedestrians—are along the sea bluffs on **West Cliff Drive** and
around **Santa Cruz Harbor**.

The **University of California at Santa Cruz** campus has
more bicycles than cars (and more cars than parking spaces).
From the trailhead on Glenn Coolidge Drive, you can bike for
a mile across the trees and meadows in the north end of **Pogonip Open Space Preserve** and reach
Henry Cowell Redwoods State Park,
where the **Rincon Fire Road** forms the
first leg of a loop that crosses the San
Lorenzo River in the heart of the redwood forest and continues along the
Ridge Fire Road and the **Powder Mill
Fire Road**. The five-mile route leaves
you on Graham Hill Road at the southeast corner of the state park—and on the
other side of the river from the trailhead,
with no bridge for miles around. Unless
you can arrange for someone to pick you
up, why not take the scenic route—back
the way you came?

Biking along the Boardwalk.

Within cycling distance of Santa Cruz, mountain bikers' hearts belong to **Wilder Ranch State Park**. More than 30 miles of trails through the hills, canyons and ridges of the park's backcountry north of Route 1 are designated multiple-use for hikers, equestrians and bikers, but limited parking alongside the highway at the trailheads both keeps the trails uncrowded and gives a natural advantage to those who can ride out there without a car. The trails here are such a maze that local riders recommend daytrips like "Chinquapin to Baldwin to Enchanted to Baldwin again to Enchanted again, then along the southern Eucalyptus and down to the bottom of Old Cabin back out to northern Eucalyptus and up to Wilder Ridge, taking the Zane Grey Cutoff" (21 miles through everything from veggie fields to stark badlands to redwood forests and back). Anyone you rent a mountain bike from in Santa Cruz can offer their own version of the best ride in Wilder, along with a map. Try **Armadillo Cyclery** (1211 Mission Street; 831-426-7299) or **The Bicycle Shop** (1325 Mission Street; 831-454-0909; www.bicy cleshopsantacruz.com).

SKATING

The most popular place in town for rollerblading is the paved multiple-use trail that parallels West Cliff Drive between Santa Cruz Beach and Natural Bridges State Beach.

The largest Santa Cruz skate park is **The Fun Spot**, a 14,000-square-foot expanse of concrete featuring Ramptech vertical and street course terrain. Located just off Santa Cruz Beach, the city-owned park is open to skateboarders and inline skaters only. ~ Beach Street at Pacific Avenue; 831-420-5270. There's another skate park at **Derby Park** at the north end of San Jose Street, five blocks off West Cliff Drive. Skateboarding is allowed on weekends only at **Santa Cruz High School** (415 Walnut Street; 831-429-3959). Skaters may also want to try the **Santa Cruz Roller Palladium** (1606 Seabright Avenue; 831-423-0844), a conventional roller rink.

OPPOSITE: Biker on bluffs above Wilder Ranch State Park.

You can rent or buy skates and safety equipment at **Go Skate, Surf & Sport, Inc.** (601 Beach Street; 831-425-0844) and **Skateworks** (129 Bulkhead Street; 831-427-4292; www.skateworks.com).

DIVING

To explore the rock walls and reefs that lie hidden just beneath the ocean's surface off the Santa Cruz coast, head for **Ocean Odyssey International Dive Center**, where scuba instructors offer lessons for individuals of all skill levels, and organize Monterey Bay Marine Sanctuary dive excursions, including five- to six-hour charter trips and night dives. Closed on Tuesday. ~ 860 17th Avenue; 831-475-3483; www.oceanodyssey.com, e-mail staff @oceanodyssey.com.

Adventure Sports Unlimited's instructors teach beginning scuba techniques in a pool heated to tropical temperatures before sending you off with a certified dive master to experience the undersea wonders of the bay. They also rent and sell scuba gear. ~ 303 Potrero Court #15; 831-458-3648, 888-839-4286; www.asudoit.com, e-mail asudoit@asudoit.com.

Aqua Safaris SCUBA Center offers diving and safety instruction, equipment rentals, tank gas fills and Monterey Bay dive excursions. ~ 6896-A Soquel Avenue; 831-479-4386; www.aquasafaris.com.

WHERE KITES FLY PEOPLE

The latest of those recreational inventions that seem to pour out of Santa Cruz (others have included the Frisbee, disc golf and the wet suit), kiteboarding combines windsurfing and wakeboarding techniques with huge kites like crescent-shaped parachutes, enabling riders to launch from the surf and sail up to 40 feet in the air. The place to watch kiteboarders in action is **Waddell Beach State Park**, located 16 miles north of Santa Cruz on Route 1.

SURFING

Needless to say, surfing is huge in Santa Cruz. The water may run ten degrees colder than in Southern California, but ever since local surfing champion Jack O'Neill

Surfer at Steamer Lane.

invented the wet suit, the chill hasn't deterred droves of novice and expert surfers alike from pitting their skill and nerve against the West Coast's most spectacular waves and breaks.

The "bunny slope" of Santa Cruz surfing is **Cowell's**, the water just off Cowell Beach between Santa Cruz Beach and Lighthouse Point. The waves here are easy enough to make it ideal for classes that get beginners standing up on their boards the first day. The angle of the shoreline allows for rides that are not only gentle but very long—sometimes more than a mile.

Adjacent to Cowell's on the east side of Lighthouse Point, **Steamer Lane** has been called the classic surf break in the world. Four reef breaks roll into one spot to create waves that not only provide an ideal site for one of surfing's top championship competitions but also endless entertainment for camera-clicking spectators atop the cliffs near the surfing museum.

On the east side of Santa Cruz, popular **Pleasure Point** is a thrill ride that surfers of all skill levels tackle with all kinds of equipment from longboards and rippers to boogieboards. It's no accident that local legend Jack O'Neill, who is credited with bringing the sport to Santa Cruz in the first place, chose Pleasure Point as the location for his house. The point is off East Cliff Drive midway between Santa Cruz and Capitola beaches.

West of town, surfing sites are small and numerous, and everyone seems to have his or her secret favorite. To start with, **Natural Bridges State Beach** develops spectacular eight-foot tubes when conditions are just right. Other good spots a little farther up the coast, known as **Three Mile** and **Four Mile** for the distances from Santa Cruz, offer exciting reef breaks and are usually less crowded because reaching them requires lugging your board a fair distance through fields of Brussels sprouts.

Santa Cruz's original surfing school, the **Richard Schmidt Surf School** has been in operation since 1978. Its founder, an internationally renowned big-wave rider, guarantees that each student will stand and surf on the first lesson day. Private and

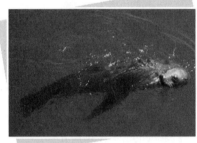
Sea lion.

group classes are available, as well as week-long surf camps. ~ 236 San Jose Avenue; 831-423-0928; www.richardschmidt. com, e-mail info@richard schmidt.com.

The other famous-name surfing school in Santa Cruz, **Club Ed** was founded by Ed Guzman, who coached the championship U.S. Army surfing team at Fort Ord for seven years before becoming the head instructor for the University of California at Santa Cruz surfing program. He opened his own school, which offers private and group instruction, including all-women classes, and conducts surf camps in summer on Monterey Bay and down the Pacific coast in Baja California in winter and spring. Club Ed also rents boards and wet suits. ~ 5 Isbel Drive; 831-459-9283, 800-287-7873, fax 831-427-9283; www.club-ed.com, e-mail clubed@sbcglobal.net.

Board and wet-suit rentals and surfing instruction are also available at **Cowell's Beach 'n' Bikini Surf Shop** (30 Front Street; 831-427-2355), **Freeline Design** (821 41st Avenue; 831-476-2950; www.freelinesurf.com) and **O'Neill Beach Store** (2222 East Cliff Drive; 831-376-5200).

For 24-hour surf condition reports, call 831-475-2275.

FISHING

Charter operators take anglers out on the bay to fish for chinook salmon (April through October), albacore (August through October) and cod and snapper (May through February). The longest-established charter service in town, in business since 1879, is **Stagnaro's Sportfishing**. ~ 32 Santa Cruz Municipal Wharf; 831-427-2334, fax 831-427-0764; www. stagnaros.com. Other deep-sea fishing charter operators include **Santa Cruz Sportfishing, Inc.** (Upper Santa Cruz Harbor, Dock H; 831-426-4960; www.santacruzsportfishing.com) and **Scurfield's Landing/Shamrock Charters** (2210 East Cliff Drive; 831-476-2648; www.scurfslanding.com).

Those who wish to do their fishing from terra firma can cast their lines from the **Santa Cruz Municipal Pier** or fish the surf from any of innumerable rocky points along the coast.

Common catches include rock-fish, surf perch and halibut. Tidepools are good places for crabbing and poke-pole fishing for eels. Anglers age 16 and over must have a California fishing license unless fishing from a municipal pier. Both one-day and annual licenses are available from local bait

Red snapper is a prized fish along the California Coast.

and tackle shops such as **Andy's Bait & Tackle Shop** (Municipal Pier; 831-429-1925) and **Bayside Marine** (333 Lake Avenue; 831-475-2173; www.baysidemarinesc.com).

WHALE WATCHING

Whale watching reaches its peak in January, February and March, when more than 20,000 gray whales pass Santa Cruz and Monterey Bay on their migration from Alaska to the calving lagoons of Baja California and back. Whale-watching tours are also offered in summer, when humpback and blue whales sometimes visit the deep waters of Monterey Bay, though passengers are more likely to see sea otters, sea lions and dolphins.

Summer and winter whale-watching charters are offered by **Stagnaro's Sportfishing** (32 Santa Cruz Municipal Wharf; 831-427-2334, fax 831-427-0764; www.stagnaros.com) and **Scurfield's Landing/Shamrock Charters** (2210 East Cliff Drive; 831-476-2648; www.scurfslanding.com). **Chardonnay Sailing Charters** (790 Mariner Parkway; 831-423-1213, fax 831-427-5046; www.chardonnay.com) offers luxury whale-watching charters on a 70-foot sailing yacht, and **Lighthall Yacht Charters** (934 Bay Street; 831-429-1970; www.lighthallcharters.com) sets out on a 42-foot yacht in search of whales on its regularly scheduled "marine ecology sails."

Whales are rarely seen from the shore in Santa Cruz or elsewhere along the shore of Monterey Bay. To whale watch from terra firma, drive nine miles north on Route 1 to the old whaling village of **Davenport**, where—for reasons unknown—migrating gray whales come closer to shore than anywhere else on the coast. The prime whale-watching spot is on the bluffs overlooking the sea across from Ocean Street. Bring binoculars.

 ## KAYAKING

Kayakers enjoy exploring the coves and kelp forests in the Santa Cruz Municipal Pier and Lighthouse Point areas. **Venture Quest Kayaking** rents kayaks, complete with wet suit and gear, by the hour or day. The company also offers lessons and guided moonlight outings and half-day and full-day nature tours to watch sea lions, sea otters and—if you're lucky—whales. ~ 125 Beach Street; 831-427-2267; www.kayak santacruz.com. **Kayak Connection** offers guided nature trips by kayak to various locations around Monterey Bay, including overnight trips to Elkhorn Slough. ~ 413 Lake Avenue #4; 831-479-1121; www.kayakconnection.com. Tours and instruction are also available at **Adventure Sports Unlimited** (303 Potrero Court #15; 831-458-3648, 888-839-4286; www.asudoit.

com) and **Santa Cruz Paddle Sports** (P.O. Box 815, Felton, CA 95018; 831-252-8116; www.santacruzpaddlesports.com).

RIDING STABLES

Popular areas for horseback riding are **Wilder Ranch State Park**, where all trails north of Route 1 are open to equestrians, and **Henry Cowell Redwoods State Park**, where horses are allowed on all trails except the Redwood Grove Trail, Meadow Trail, Ox Trail and Pipeline Road south of Rincon Fire Road.

Unless you bring your own horses in a trailer, you'll find that horse rentals in the Santa Cruz area are limited to guided rides, mostly through the forests surrounding the village of Felton north of town. Try **Twin Oaks Farm** (600 McEnery Road, Felton; 831-335-2929), **Chaparral Corral** (122 Covered Bridge Road, Felton; 831-335-1887), **Horse Haven Ranch** (7940 East Zayante Road, Felton; 831-335-1887), **Wingspan Stables** (5423 Route 9, Felton; 831-335-9464), **Redwood Riding Adventures** (P.O. Box 236, Felton, CA 95018; 831-335-1334) or **Loma Alta Farm** (3300 Stable Lane, Santa Cruz; 831-476-3335).

GOLF

Set in the hills overlooking Santa Cruz, the 18-hole **Pasatiempo Golf Club** links date back to 1929 and still ranks high on every list of top U.S. golf courses. Legendary golf course designer Alister MacKenzie, who also created such famous courses as Cypress Point on the Monterey Peninsula, said that the 6154-yard par-72 Pasatiempo was his most beloved design and that its 16th hole—a par-4 dogleg left—was his best work ever; MacKenzie chose to build his final home overlooking it. According to the clubhouse guest register, celebrity duffers such as Jack Dempsey, Ty Cobb, Bing Crosby and Tiger Woods have played here. Club and cart rentals are available. ~ 20 Clubhouse Road; 831-459-9169, fax 831-426-0739; www.pasatiempo.com.

Also located in the hills above town, the park-like, 18-hole municipal **DeLaveaga Golf Course** was built in 1970 by Bert Stamps. At 6010 yards, the par-72 course is short, tight and full of forest hazards and slopes. Cart and club rentals are available. ~ 401 Upper Park Road; 831-423-7212; www.delaveaga golf.com.

 ## CAMPING

There is no waterfront camping in the immediate Santa Cruz vicinity. Campers who prefer to drift off to sleep to the sound of the surf usually opt to stay at state park beaches farther south along the bay (see Chapter 3).

About four miles north of town on Graham Hill Road (which forks off Ocean Street just north of the junction of Routes 1 and 17), **Henry Cowell Redwoods State Park** has 112 quiet tent/RV sites surrounded by tall, shady forest. Hiking trails to all parts of the 1800-acre park start at or near the campground. Located near the northeast corner of the state park's main unit, the campground has restrooms and pay showers; sites have picnic tables and grills but no hookups. Sites cost $16 to $20 per night. Closed December to mid-February. ~ Graham Hill Road; 831-335-4598, reservations 800-444-7275; www.reserve america.com.

RVers who crave the convenience of full hookups and resort amenities will find them at the privately run **Smithwoods RV Park**, located seven miles north of downtown Santa Cruz near the main entrance to Henry Cowell Redwoods State Park. There are 142 RV sites on concrete pads (no tent camping), all with picnic tables, grills and water, electric and sewer hookups. Besides restrooms and showers, campground amenities include a swimming pool, a kids' playground, a game room and a camping store. There are even modem connections for your laptop. Sites cost $36 per night. Open year-round. ~ Route 9; 831-335-4321.

About ten miles northwest of Santa Cruz off Route 1 (look for the patriotic mailbox), privately owned and clothing-optional **Red, White and Blue Beach** has 28 tent sites and a section for self-contained vehicles but no hookups. There are picnic areas, a volleyball court, restrooms, showers and security "rangers." No fires on the beach, dogs or cameras. Sites cost $18 per person, first-come, first-served. Campground closed November through January. Day-use fee, $12. ~ Scaroni Road; phone/fax 831-423-6332.

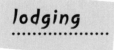

lodging

Santa Cruz has a number of vintage motels within walking distance of the Boardwalk. Don't expect much in the way of decor, but if a bed, shower, phone, TV and a little privacy to change into and out of your bathing suit are all you need, look no further. Rates at most of these establishments are in the moderate range in summer and drop into the budget range the rest of the year.

One good bet, the **Charles Court** is in a quiet location and has a pool and somewhat more presentable furniture than that found at most of the other beach motels. ~ 902 3rd Street; 831-423-2091. BUDGET TO MODERATE.

Another modest but attractive lodging near the beach, the 34-unit **Carousel Motel** has spacious, well-furnished rooms with pastel decor, flowered bedspreads and private balconies. Special packages combine two nights' lodging and two un-limited ride passes for the Boardwalk. ~ 110 Riverside Avenue; 831-425-7090, 800-214-7400, fax 831-423-4801. BUDGET TO MODERATE.

A block from the beach, the **Beach View Inn** has 22 nicely furnished standard motel units (some with whirlpool baths) and off-street parking. ~ 50 Front Street; 831-426-3575, 800-946-0614, fax 831-421-9218; www.beach-viewinn.com, e-mail reser vations@beach-viewinn.com. BUDGET TO DELUXE.

Not all the lodgings around the central beach area are funky or motel-ish, however. Located at the base of Beach Hill, the **Château Victorian Bed & Breakfast Inn** is a Queen Anne Revival–style mansion with seven sunny guest rooms, each with a queen-size bed, fireplace, private bath and plush carpeting.

••
Sleep Like a Millionaire

In the early years of the 20th century, the stretch of West Cliff Drive between Cow-ell Beach and Lighthouse Point was dubbed Millionaire's Row because it was lined with lavish estates. Some (such as the grand mansion that was razed to create the park at Lighthouse Point) no longer exist; others were subdivided among family members who built new generations of mansions side-by-side with the old. And some of these mansions have been converted into luxury bed-and-breakfast inns. A prime example is the **Darling House Bed & Breakfast by the Sea**, a 1910 archi-tectural masterpiece overlooking Cowell Beach and the Santa Cruz Municipal Pier. The distant screams of thrilled rollercoaster riders on the Boardwalk blend with sounds of surf and birds to create a symphony wafting through the peaceful lawn, citrus orchard, grape arbor, flower gardens and palm trees that surround the house. Inside, the common areas and guest rooms are filled with fresh-cut flowers, polished dark hardwood fittings, antique furnishings, Tiffany lamps and beveled and stained-glass windows. Most, but not all, rooms have ocean views, fireplaces and private baths. ~ 314 West Cliff Drive; 831-458-1958; www.darlinghouse.com, e-mail ddarling@darlinghouse.com.
••

Coast Santa Cruz Hotel.

Antique furnishings throughout give the inn a museum-like feel. The owner, who lives on the premises, each morning serves an expanded continental breakfast of fresh pastries from one of Santa Cruz's best bakeries. ~ 118 1st Street; 831-458-9458; www.chateauvictorian.com. MODERATE TO DELUXE.

Nearby on Beach Hill, yet at the low end of the price spectrum, **Hostelling International—Santa Cruz** youth hostel offers dorm-style accommodations for 40 guests, as well as two private rooms for families. The shared baths have hot showers, and guests get kitchen privileges. Bring a sleeping bag or rent sheets. Three-night maximum stay in summer and an 11 p.m. curfew year-round. ~ 321 Main Street; 831-423-8304, 800-909-4776 ext. 45, fax 831-429-8541; www.hi-santacruz.org, e-mail info@hi-santacruz.org. BUDGET.

Santa Cruz is conspicuous in its lack of the kind of high-rise sea-view hotels typical of many beach resorts. About the closest thing you'll find is the 163-unit, ten-story **Coast Santa Cruz Hotel**, right on Cowell Beach. The rooms feature contemporary furnishings and fabric-covered walls along with such little niceties as hairdryers, irons, safes and closed-circuit video games. Each unit has a private balcony with a view of the ocean and municipal pier. There's a heated outdoor swimming pool and a large whirlpool hot tub. ~ 175 West Cliff Drive; 831-426-4330, 800-663-1144, fax 831-427-2025; www.coastho tels.com. DELUXE TO ULTRA-DELUXE.

Some of the old mansions along the part of West Cliff Drive once known as Millionaires' Row have been converted to elegant bed and breakfasts. Among the most stately is the **Cliff Crest Bed &Breakfast Inn**, an 1887 Queen Anne Victorian set on grounds landscaped with redwoods, lilacs, bamboo and jasmine by the designer of San Francisco's Golden Gate Park. Each of the five period-furnished guest rooms has a private bath, some with clawfoot tubs. Most have ocean views, and one unit has a fireplace. Full breakfast included. ~ 407 Cliff Street; 831-427-2609, fax 831-427-2710; www.cliffcrestbedandbreak fast.com, e-mail info@cliffcrestbedandbreakfast.com. MODERATE TO ULTRA-DELUXE.

Its location, near a quiet neighborhood beach well removed from the mainstream of tourist activity, makes the **Ocean Echo Inn & Beach Cottages** a special find for solitude seekers. Some of the 15 studios and Cape Cod–style cottages have kitchens and private patios. Two-night minimum in summer; weekly rates are available. ~ 401 Johans Beach Drive; 831-462-4192, fax 831-462-0658; www.oceanecho.com, e-mail beach@ocean echo.com. MODERATE.

Another friendly accommodation in a residential neighborhood a short walk from a local beach, the two-story stucco

Cliff Crest Bed & Breakfast Inn.

Harbor Inn has 19 attractive guest rooms, all spacious and simply furnished. All units have refrigerators and microwaves. ~

645 7th Avenue; 831-479-9731, fax 831-479-1067; www.harborinnsan tacruz.com. MODERATE.

One of the most luxurious lodgings in Santa Cruz, the **Pleasure Point Inn** sits on the edge of the cliffs overlooking a popular surfing break midway between Santa Cruz Beach and Capitola. The inn is ultramodern inside and out, with architecture that integrates Mediterranean, art deco and nautical elements. The living room and dining area have high beam ceilings and polished hardwood floors, and the five guest

View from Ocean Echo Inn & Beach Cottages.

rooms are individually decorated with custom-made light wood furnishings. All rooms have gas fireplaces, ocean views, private patios and digital cable TV. The large rooftop deck has chaises longues and an eight-person hot tub with a view of the bay. Complete massage and spa services are available on-site. ~ 2-3665 East Cliff Drive; 831-475-4657, 877-557-2567; www. pleasurepointinn.com. ULTRA-DELUXE.

dining

In downtown Santa Cruz, **El Palomar** specializes in gourmet regional Mexican food featuring fresh local seafood and handmade tortillas. Top off a dinner of grilled red snapper tacos or chicken in an unusual, tasty *mole poblano* sauce with a mango margarita. The setting is the high-ceilinged, colorfully muraled dining room of a vintage hotel from the 1930s. ~ 1336 Pacific Avenue; 831-425-7575, fax 831-426-1720. MODERATE.

Benten, a simply decorated Japanese restaurant and sushi bar, serves a tempting selection of traditional Japanese fare. The menu includes tempura, teriyaki, *yosenabe* and sashimi entrées as well as *khaki* fry—deep-fried breaded oysters. Closed

Tuesday. ~ 1541 Pacific Avenue, Suite B; 831-425-7079. BUD-
GET TO MODERATE

One of Santa Cruz's most elegant restaurants, **Oswald**
serves haute cuisine with a European accent in an intimate
bistro-style setting. Representative menu items include braised
rabbit, *spaetzle* and peach chutney. Round out your meal with
a choice of fantastic desserts and a selection from the impeccable wine list. ~ 1547 Pacific Avenue; 831-423-7427. DELUXE.

Judging from its name, you might expect the **Casa Blanca
Restaurant** to serve Mexican food, but in fact its Moroccan-
style decor suggests that it was named for Casablanca (the city
or maybe the movie), though the real Casablanca has nothing
remotely like the wraparound view of the ocean that diners here
enjoy. There's nothing particularly North African about the
menu, which features entrées like seafood linguini, grilled
duck and brandied filet mignon. Dinner only. ~ 101 Main
Street; 831-426-9063; www.casablanca-santacruz.com, e-mail
casabeach@aol.com. DELUXE.

Three blocks from the Santa Cruz Farmers' Market, the
Gabriella Café uses only fresh local organic produce, and its
menu changes seasonally. Typical fare might be an appetizer
of crab and squash cakes followed by a guinea hen with tar-
ragon sauce, roasted figs and root vegetables along with the
house's special homemade focaccia bread. Sparkling white

El Palomar.

tablecloths, stucco archways and a profusion of freshly cut flowers help create the restaurant's romantic ambience. ~ 910 Cedar Street; 831-457-1677; www.gabriellacafe.com. DELUXE.

Down by Santa Cruz Beach, the **Ideal Bar and Grille** is a far cry from the carnival-style hot-dog stands that line the Boardwalk nearby. In business since 1917 in its hole-in-the-wall location between the beach and the pier, its outdoor deck reaches out onto the sand. The fare focuses on seafood—lobster, calamari, salmon, oysters and more. ~ 106 Beach Street; 831-423-5271, fax 831-423-3827. MODERATE TO DELUXE.

Over the river and a mile east of downtown, a little diner and take-out place known as **Charlie Hong Kong** is a local favorite for its healthy, organic renditions of Asian street-style cuisine such as Vietnamese sandwiches, Thai coconut mushroom soup, teriyaki salmon and spicy vegetarian *gado gado*. ~ 1141 Soquel Avenue; 831-426-5664; www.charliehongkong.com, e-mail rudy@charliehongkong.com. BUDGET TO MODERATE.

The number of restaurants is burgeoning in the area around the Santa Cruz Small Craft Harbor. One longtime local favorite for breakfast and lunch, **Aldo's Harbor Restaurant** near Seabright Beach serves up an assortment of soups, salads, sandwiches and seafood dishes indoors or on an outdoor deck. ~ 616 Atlantic Avenue; 831-426-3736, fax 831-426-1362. BUDGET TO MODERATE

Ideal Bar and Grille.

●●●
Shop Fresh, Eat Healthy
Rural areas of Santa Cruz County have long been the domain of independent
farmers who grow specialized organic produce. In 1990, when the Santa Cruz
Downtown Association hit upon the strategy of starting a farmers' market to
bring people back downtown after the devastating Loma Prieta earthquake, both
growers and shoppers greeted the idea with such enthusiasm that it now takes
place weekly year-round. In the winter, fruits and vegetables are brought in from
certified organic farms in other parts of California. There are also homemade
baked goods, preserves and other picnic fixings. **The Santa Cruz Farmers' Market**
is held from 2:30 to 6:30 p.m. every Wednesday at the intersection of Lincoln and
Cedar streets. Many of the same vendors can also be found at other Santa Cruz
County farmers' markets in Felton (Felton Presbyterian Church, Tuesdays 2:30 to
6:30 p.m., May through November), Watsonville (Peck and Main streets, Fridays
3 to 7 p.m.) and Aptos (Cabrillo College parking lots B, C and D, Saturdays 8 a.m.
to noon).
●●●

The most popular spot at the harbor, the beachfront **Crow's
Nest Restaurant** is located directly under the Coast Guard lookout tower (or "crow's nest" in nautical lingo). Natural wood
beams and pillars and crisp white tablecloths, plus panoramic
views that take in the whole bay from Lighthouse Point south
to the lights of Monterey, set the tone in the main downstairs
dining area. Among the entrées are chargrilled albacore kabobs
marinated in Szechuan sauce, Australian lobster tail, sirloin
hatsui (Japanese-style marinated lean beef) and, for vegetari-
ans, pasta with portobello mushrooms, sun-dried tomatoes and
toasted pine nuts. No lunch on weekends. On the second story,
with the same management and a more casual menu, the
Breakwater Bar & Grill serves burgers, wings, fish-and-chips
and fried calamari all day, every day. ~ 2218 East Cliff Drive;
831-476-4560; www.crowsnest-santacruz.com, e-mail info@
crowsnest-santacruz.com. MODERATE

Still going strong after nearly three decades, **The
Catalyst**'s main music hall hosts heavyweight
Bay Area bands on weekends while local groups
perform on weeknights in the atrium. The ros-
ter of musicians who have performed here over the years reads

nightlife
●●●●●●●●●●●●●●●●●

Sample of Victorian architecture in Santa Cruz.

like a history of rock-and-roll—the Byrds, Buffalo Springfield, Santana, Bo Diddley, Jefferson Airplane, Tina Turner, Jerry Garcia, Bonnie Raitt, R.E.M., The Band, Janis Joplin and hundreds more. Cover for live music. ~ 1011 Pacific Avenue; 831-423-7853; www.catalystclub.com.

Nationally known blues acts take the stage nightly at **Moe's Alley Blues Club**. Regular performers include Clarence "Gatemouth" Brown, Coco Montoya and Debbie Davies. Cover. ~ 1535 Commercial Way; 831-479-1845; www.moes alley.com.

At Santa Cruz Harbor, the **Crow's Nest** presents an wide range of entertainment including live salsa, reggae, rock, blues and jazz, as well as stand-up comics on Sunday nights. ~ 2218 East Cliff Drive; 831-476-4560; www.crowsnest-santacruz.com, e-mail info@crowsnest-santacruz.com.

On the mellow side, the **Kuumbwa Jazz Center** headlines top-name musicians. Cover. ~ 320 Cedar Street; 831-427-2227; www.jazzqwest.com/kuumbwa.

Even mellower, the **Jahva House** serves soy lattes and vegetarian snacks to patrons of all ages relaxing on couches beneath hanging plants. It presents live music occasionally. ~ 120 Union Street; 831-423-2053.

Santa Cruz has an extraordinarily lively and diverse theater scene for a town its size. Foremost is **Shakespeare in Santa**

Cruz, presented by the University of California at Santa Cruz during the summer months on an outdoor stage surrounded by redwoods. The plays always sell out, so advance tickets are essential. ~ 1156 High Street; 831-459-2121.

The huge **Santa Cruz Civic Auditorium** hosts everything from plays and concerts to art and wine festivals. ~ 307 Church Street; 831-420-5260; www.santacruzcivic.com. Another major performing-arts venue is the **Rio Theatre**, a former grand movie palace that was restored and reopened to present plays, concerts and one-person shows. ~ 1205 Soquel Avenue; 831-423-8309; www.riotheatre.com. The **Art League/Broadway Playhouse** presents productions by several community theater groups. ~ 526 Broadway; 831-426-5787. And experimental theater works hit the boards at **Actors' Theatre**. ~ 1001 Center Street; 831-425-7529; www.sccat.org.

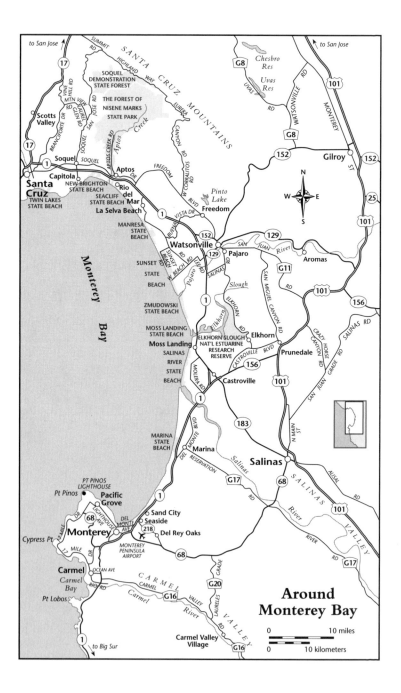

Around
Monterey Bay

0   10 miles

0   10 kilometers

Around Monterey Bay

$\mathcal{R}$oute 1, the spectacularly scenic two-lane highway that traces the California coast for hundreds of miles, becomes a hectic divided freeway as it zips around the coast of Monterey Bay, carrying motorists from Santa Cruz to Monterey in about 45 minutes. This chapter reveals what you'll miss if you take the quick route: some of California's best beaches, as well as towering redwood forests, roadside produce stands, and quaint villages devoted to fishing, antiques and even artichokes.

Travelers will quickly discover the dollar value of a great location; lodgings in the area tend to be expensive, almost all in the deluxe or ultra-deluxe price range. On the other hand, meal prices—especially at seafood eateries—are often surprisingly low. And if you're

camping, you'll find the best options in the Santa Cruz–Monterey region along these beaches.

The natural beauty of the California coast is a constant presence (except when the fog rolls in and you can't see it). Sandy beaches run virtually the entire length of the shoreline from Santa Cruz to the Monterey Peninsula. The remarkable thing is that no two stretches of beach are quite the same. Some are backed by forested bluffs. Others are amazingly wide. Still others have grassy sand dunes that stand 20 feet tall. The only natural area along the coast that doesn't have sand is Elkhorn Slough, a remarkable wildlife preserve home to hundreds of kinds of birds, along with abundant sea otters.

Outdoor activities take center stage in this area. Naturally enough, there's great surfing and fishing. It's a pleasant surprise to discover the many great hiking and biking trails in the forest just a few miles inland, and kayaking is excellent at Elkhorn Slough, where you can often watch sea otters paddling along on their backs almost within arm's reach. In the shadow of the legendary links on the Monterey Peninsula, the golf courses in this area go practically unnoticed but offer a combination of great scenery, challenging terrain, affordable fees, and easy-to-get tee times.

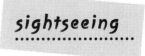

sightseeing

Located four miles southeast of Santa Cruz along the Monterey Bay shore, the artsy little village of **Capitola** lays claim to being California's oldest seaside resort. Its wharf was built around 1850 to ship produce from Watsonville area farms, and in 1870 a summer complex of tent cabins became an instant favorite among vacationers from San Francisco. To find out more about Capitola's colorful past (the fictional 1850s heroine for whom the village was named, the old resort hotel built by a survivor of the ill-fated Donner Party, the 1929 fire that burned Capitola to the ground), visit the cute **Capitola Historical Museum**, housed in what used to be a farm cottage but was remodeled to look like a little red schoolhouse. Open Friday, Saturday and Sunday afternoons. ~ 410 Capitola Avenue, Capitola; 831-464-6322; www.capitolamuseum.org, e-mail swiftcj@pacbell.net.

Capitola City Beach vanished in 1964, when the dredging of Santa Cruz Small Craft Harbor shifted the water currents in Monterey Bay. Since its reconstruction, the beach is so wide and smooth that it is often called the best beach in California. Besides the long public pier, there are restrooms, showers, life-

Public pier in Capitola.

guards and a sand volleyball court; small seafood restaurants front the beach. ~ Capitola; 831-475-7300, fax 831-479-8879.

Just south of Capitola, **New Brighton State Beach** is popular among swimmers and novice surfers because of the headlands that protect it from rough seas. It's also a favorite clam-digging spot. Facilities include picnic areas, fire pits and restrooms. Day-use fee. ~ Capitola; 831-464-6330, fax 831-685-6443.

Adjoining New Brighton State Beach, the small **Seacliff State Beach** presents the only opportunity most visitors will ever have to see a genuine concrete shipwreck. At the end of the public pier, protected by a locked chain-link gate, it's referred to locally as the "Old Cement Boat." Officially christened the SS *Palo Alto,* it was built in San Francisco during the World War I era (when steel was scarce) as part of a government experiment to ascertain the feasibility of non-steel ships, but only sailed once under its own power. In 1930, after having been moored at several piers up and down the central coast, it was towed to Capitola in 1930 to serve as an "offshore" nightclub and casino. It broke in half and sank in a storm two years later. The beach itself is said to be the safest place on Monterey Bay for swimming, with a protective headland and lifeguards. Park rangers offer guided walks to the cliffs above the beach to look at fossils. Facilities include picnic areas and restrooms, and the pier is a popular fishing spot. Day-use fee. ~ Capitola; 831-464-6330, fax 831-685-6443.

OPPOSITE: New Brighton State Beach.

A short distance inland from Capitola, on the other side of Route 1, **Soquel** got its start 150 years ago as a company town for a beet-sugar refinery. Today it's an old-fashioned-looking village with big oak trees and a classic whitewashed church steeple. Soquel is now known for its antique shops—there are more here than in any other Monterey Bay area community.

••••••••••••••••••••••••••••
Along Monterey Bay's eastern coast-line, local people often make the dis-tinction between "South County" and "North County," the dividing line being just north of the fishing village of Moss Landing. The tricky part is that the northern half of the coast is South County, and the southern half is North County—referring to Santa Clara County and Monterey County respectively.
••••••••••••••••••••••••••••

You can follow Soquel Drive south across the Cabrillo College campus to **Aptos**, gateway to The Forest of Nisene Marks State Park (see "Hiking" and "Biking" below). Aptos, too, has a history-packed past. Built as a railhead for shipping redwood logs clearcut from the forests just past the edge of town, it later became an apple-growing and -processing center. Unfortunately, its Victorian-era historic district was demolished by the 1989 Loma Prieta earthquake, except for the landmark Bayview Hotel, which was remarkably spared and continues to operate as it has since 1878. To learn more, visit the **Aptos History Museum**, located in the Chamber of Commerce building. Open weekends only. ~ 7605-A Old Dominion Court, Aptos; 831-688-1467.

A fascinating spot for plant enthusiasts is the **Bamboo Giant Nursery**, the largest U.S. supplier of bamboo for gardening and live privacy fences. Forty different species of bamboo tower over three walking trails through 15 acres of demonstration gardens. ~ 5601 Freedom Boulevard, Aptos; 831-687-0100, fax 831-687-0200; www.bamboogiant.com, e-mail info@bamboogiant.com.

For a scenic alternative between Aptos and Watsonville, follow Soquel Drive south to Freedom Boulevard. Turn right, go over Route 1 and turn left on Bonita Drive. Continue for about a mile to San Andreas Road, which glides through shady forest and then breaks out into an expanse of farm fields stretching from the sea to the mountains. Along the way, you'll see **Manresa State Beach**, a long, clean, usually uncrowded stretch of sand washed by surf that has a notorious reputation for rip currents. There are restrooms and picnic areas; lifeguards stand watch during summer. Day-use fee. ~ San Andreas Road; 831-761-1795.

On the other side of San Andreas Road, the **Long-Toed Salamander Ecological Reserve** encompasses 200 acres that make up one of the few known habitats for a little amphibian that was one of the first animals granted protection under the Endangered Species Act of 1976; it's virtually impossible to get a glimpse of one, though, since they live underground. ~ 916-653-7664.

A little farther south, **Sunset State Beach** has more than three miles of sand and dunes backed by bluffs, Monterey pines and cypress trees, making it one of the bay's prettiest beaches.

••
Fresh-picked Pleasure

Picking fruit is part of the California experience. John Steinbeck wrote about the dustbowl Okies who did it in the 1930s. Cesar Chavez brought it to national at-

tention again in the 1960s. Now you can try it, too, by visiting **Gizdich Ranch** in Watsonville, where the same family has been growing apples and berries since the era of *The Grapes of Wrath.* What may still be a hellish career for agricultural workers turns out to be a guilty pleasure for an hour or two, especially for families with grade school–age children. Gizdich Ranch's "Pik-Yor-Sef" fields and orchards are busiest during strawberry season (May through July) and apple season (late August through January 1st). You can also pick boysenberries starting in mid-June and raspberries in July, or go for olallieberries— little-known plump, dark, sweet little berries that are a hybrid of blackberries, loganberries and youngberries—also in June. You only pay for what you pick—at pretty much supermar-

ket prices. There's no extra charge for the experience. ~ 55 Peckham Road, Watsonville; 831-722-1056; www.gizdichranch.com.
••

• •
Why a National Marine Sanctuary?

As you gaze out over the waters of Monterey Bay, use your imagination to take in the fact that one of the most unusual geological formations on earth—an underwater canyon twice as deep as the Grand Canyon—lies beneath the water's surface just offshore, inviting deep-water fish to approach closer to shore than at any other place on the U.S. coastline. In addition, the bay marks the cusp of two biodiversity zones and hosts wildlife species from both the cold north Pacific and the warmer waters to the south, including 25 endangered species. These unique qualities justified the decision in 1992 to create the **Monterey Bay National Marine Sanctuary**, placing it under the protection of the National Oceanic and Atmospheric Administration. The sanctuary also includes coastal waters to the north and south, from the Golden Gate Bridge all the way to Hearst Castle, as well as the watersheds of 11 rivers that flow into it. It's the largest U.S. marine sanctuary and the second-largest protected marine area in the world, larger than either Yosemite or Yellowstone National Park, encompassing a total area of 5312 square miles. The multiple-use sanctuary allows commercial and recreational fishing, along with shipping lanes and military activities. So what does the bay's sanctuary status actually protect it from? Oil and gas drilling, along with ocean dumping, drilling and mining of the sea bed. It also creates tighter restrictions against pollution of the rivers that flow into the bay. ~ 299 Foam Street, Suite D, Monterey; 408-647-4201; bonita.mbnms.nos.noaa.gov.
• •

Facilities include picnic areas and restrooms. Day-use fee. ~ San Andreas Road; 831-763-7063, fax 831-763-7120.

San Andreas Road curves around to the left to become West Beach Road, crosses Route 1 and heads directly into **Watsonville**, a largely Latino farming community that is the commercial center for the Pajaro Valley, famed as the world's biggest producer of strawberries. A brochure with directions for a self-guided walk around the historic district, with its Victorian-era houses, is available at the **William H. Volck Museum**, which exhibits an extensive collection of household items from the late-19th and early-20th centuries. ~ Beach Street at Lincoln Street, Watsonville; 831-722-0305.

The **Agricultural History Project Museum**, a permanent fixture at the Santa Cruz County Fairgrounds, exhibits antique tractors and other farm machinery and implements. ~ 2601 East Lake Avenue, Watsonville; 831-724-5671.

Across the road from the fairgrounds, **Sierra Azul Nursery & Gardens** invites the public to stroll through its large, park-like demonstration garden full of unusual plants from other parts of the world that have climates similar to California's, including the Mediterranean area, South Africa and coastal Australia. ~ 2660 East Lake Avenue, Watsonville; 831-763-0939; www.sierraazul.com, e-mail sierrarosendale@compuserve.com.

Roses of Yesterday and Today, a privately owned garden and nursery established in the 1930s, displays an astonishing variety of old, rare and unusual roses. Some date back to the 16th century, while others have enchanting names such as the Newport fairy rose, the white dawn rose and the honey sweet rose. ~ 803 Brown's Valley Road, Watsonville; 831-728-1901; www.rosesofyesterday.com, e-mail postmaster@rosesofyesterday.com.

Back across Route 1, a long stretch of sand and dunes is divided into three separate beaches (**Zmudowski State Beach**, **Moss Landing State Beach** and **Salinas River State Beach**) with different names because they have different entrances. The magical ambience created by the rolling sand dunes is marred somewhat by their proximity to the enormous smokestacks of Moss Landing's power plant. All three beaches have restrooms, though no other facilities. There's a day-use fee at Moss Landing State Beach; no charge at the others. ~ Off Route 1, Moss Landing; 831-384-7695.

Despite the power plant, the little village of **Moss Landing** is a charmer with its colorful fishing fleet, weatherbeaten

Black-necked stilt.

wood fish market, one-lane bridge and old-fashioned main street packed with antique dealers. For lovers of nature, the area's main attraction is **Elkhorn Slough National Estuarine Research Reserve**, 1400 acres of tidal flats and wetlands that change back

• •

A Harvest of Festivities

Many farm communities in the Monterey Bay area are known for their specialty crops, and most of them sponsor town celebrations when harvest time rolls around. Fruit and veggie enthusiasts take note. The annual **Artichoke Festival** (831-633-2465; www.artichoke-festival.org) is held in Castroville in mid-May. The **Garlic Festival** (408-842-1625; www.gilroygarlicfestival.com) takes place in late July farther inland in Gilroy. The **Strawberry Festival** (831-728-6183; www. mbsf.com) is held in early August in Watsonville. Gizdich Ranch near Watsonville hosts the **Apple Butter Festival** (831-722-1056; www.gizdichranch.com) in mid-October. Although Carmel's exclusive Quail Lodge doesn't grow its own tomatoes, it does host the mid-September **TomatoFest** (831-620-8886; www. quaillodge.com), America's largest tomato-tasting event with over 200 varieties on display and cooking demonstrations by the area's top chefs. And of course, no list of foodfests would be complete without Santa Cruz's mid-January **Fungus Fair** (831-420-6115; www.santacruzmuseums.org).

• •

and forth between salt and fresh water with the tides, creating an environment that supports an unusually wide range of animal and plant life, including 80 species of fish and nearly 300 species of birds as well as sea otters and harbor seals. Ranger-guided tours are offered on weekends. Closed Mondays and Tuesdays. Admission. ~ 1700 Elkhorn Road, Watsonville; 831-728-2822; www.elkhornslough.org, e-mail esf@elkhornslough.org.

Past Moss Landing, Route 1 veers inland again and in three miles brings you to **Castroville**, a one-crop farming town. Driving down the main street, you'll have no trouble figuring out what that crop is: There's an artichoke motel, several artichoke-themed restaurants and cafés and even a giant artichoke sculpture in the center of town. Plan to stop for a heaping helping of deep-fried artichokes. (There's not much else to do in Castroville.)

From Castroville, consider a nine-mile detour inland on Route 183 to **Salinas**, the birthplace of Nobel Prize–winning novelist John Steinbeck, whose greatest works were set in the Monterey Bay area and who is celebrated throughout the region today although during his lifetime he was so reviled by Monterey locals that he finally moved away in disgust. The **National Steinbeck Center** originally

OPPOSITE: John Steinbeck.

Steinbeck House.

opened in 1998 as a research library housing more than 45,000 manuscripts, first editions, newspaper and magazine articles, reviews, letters, TV and radio scripts, theses and historic photographs by and about Steinbeck and his works. Anticipating the numbers of sightseers that would flock here in 2002 because of the publicity surrounding the 100th anniversary of Steinbeck's birth, the center added a range of additional features including interactive exhibits, an art gallery, a gift shop, a café and seven theaters that show film versions of Steinbeck classics including *East of Eden, The Grapes of Wrath, Of Mice and Men* and *Cannery Row.* Admission. ~ 1 Main Street, Salinas; 831-796-3833, fax 831-796-3828; www.steinbeck.org, e-mail info@steinbeck.org.

Two blocks away, the grand, turreted Victorian **Steinbeck House**, where the author was born and raised, operates as a luncheon restaurant. Tours are offered on Sundays at 1 p.m. during the summer. ~ 132 Central Avenue, Salinas; 831-424-2735; www.infopoint.com/mry/orgs/steinbeck.

At the Garden of Memories cemetery you'll find **John Steinbeck's Grave**—a poignant reminder that Steinbeck's life-long vilification by Salinas residents once drove him to observe that they would welcome him "only when I am delivered in a pine box." ~ 768 Abbot Street. From Salinas, Route 68 takes you directly to Monterey, a distance of 14 miles.

If you stay on Route 40 between Castroville and Monterey, you can visit **Marina State Beach** and see 170 acres of the tallest sand dunes on the California coast. Sunbathers, anglers, hang gliders and model airplane buffs come here to play; rip tides can make swimming treacherous. There are restrooms and a snack bar. The entrance is nine miles north of Monterey. ~ Route 1, Marina; 831-384-7695.

outdoor adventures

HIKING

Distances for hiking trails are one-way unless otherwise noted.

If Nisene Marks were mysterious glyphs carved on the trunks of redwood trees by some lost ancient civilization, **The Forest of Nisene Marks State Park** would be the natural place to search for them. In fact, though, Nisene Marks was a Dutch immigrant farmer in Aptos who bought this 10,000-acre tract of land cheap after loggers had clearcut it from the 1880s through the 1920s until only stumps remained. Noticing the

Ground Zero in the Forest

On October 17, 1989, Northern California's worst earthquake in 83 years struck the Bay Area, with its epicenter in **The Forest of Nisene Marks State Park**. It caused more than $6 billion in property damage and the loss of 62 lives, as well as 3757 injuries and damage to 18,000 homes. Hardest hit was Santa Cruz, where unreinforced brick facades along what was then known as Pacific Garden Mall (now officially redesignated "downtown Santa Cruz") collapsed; Watsonville and Moss Landing were also hard-hit. The earthquake generated a four-foot tsunami wave in Monterey Bay, touching off landslides in the undersea canyon beneath the surface of the bay. The quake resulted from the San Andreas Fault slipping as much as seven feet, but the slippage occurred so far underground that it left no trace on the earth's surface over the epicenter. If you visit The Forest of Nisene Marks State Park today, the only trace you'll see of the earthquake is a small plaque marking the epicenter.

redwood saplings that had sprung up around the stumps of forest giants, Marks decided to let the forest regenerate. When he passed away, his heirs gave the land to California as a state park on condition that it be preserved to continue its regrowth. Today, about 75 years after the clearcutting ended, the forest is filled with trees averaging 18 to 24 inches in diameter and standing as much as 200 feet tall, growing in clusters from the stumps of trees five times as big and 20 times as old. There are some 30 miles of hiking and biking trails in the park. The main route, **Aptos Creek Fire Road**, climbs 2000 feet in elevation as it winds 14.5 miles through the center of the park. It is off-

limits to motor vehicles but often busy with mountain-bike traffic that hikers may find disruptive. A dozen or more side trails are for hikers only, including the 4-mile **West Ridge Trail**, which starts at the main parking area, traverses the other side of the canyon from the Aptos Creek Fire Road and eventually connects with the fire road, making for a challenging all-day loop trip. The easier 2-mile **Rancho Aptos Trail** also starts at the main parking area and follows the slopes above a small gorge cut by Aptos Creek and runs through tall, dense redwood stands. The park may not be easy to find. No sign in Aptos marks the way to the park, and even the street sign has been altered from "Aptos Creek Rd." to simply "Aptos." Once you drive the six miles of unpaved road and pay the $1 parking fee, you'll find that plenty of other people know how to find this big, incognito state park. Start early; the parking lot at the trailhead is small, and most of Aptos Creek Road has been posted "no parking." ~ Aptos Creek Road, Aptos; 831-335-4598.

Three interconnecting loop trails wind through **Elkhorn Slough National Estuarine Research Reserve**, making for hikes of anywhere from two-and-a-half to six miles across gently rolling, grassy hills and, with the aid of boardwalks, through wetlands fringed by stands of oak and eucalyptus. All trails start from the visitors center. Shortest is the mile-long **Long Valley Loop Trail**, which takes you across a meadow and under a tunnel-like canopy of trees on its way to a "finger" of water in Parson's Slough. Those who want a longer loop can join the 2-mile **Five Fingers Loop Trail**, which circles a hammock to an overlook at the point where all five fingers of the slough converge. Nearby, a wildlife blind allows discreet viewing of the abundant bird life. A third trail, the 3.3-mile **South Marsh Loop Trail**, links with the Five Fingers Loop Trail in figure-eight fashion near the barn of the defunct Elkhorn Dairy Farm and travels on a raised pathway across the wetlands. A side trail detours to an overlook on the more remote North Marsh. ~ 1700 Elkhorn Road, Watsonville; 831-728-2822; www. elkhornslough.org, e-mail esf@elkhornslough.org.

BIKING

A heated controversy has existed between hikers and bikers for more than a decade concerning whether mountain bikes should be allowed in **The Forest of Nisene Marks State Park**. The government's compromise has been to allow mountain bikes on 15 of the 30 miles of park trails. Although they are still designated as multiple-use trails, very few equestrians ride here, and naturally enough, hikers prefer the no-bike trails with the exception of the Aptos Creek Fire Road, the park's main route connecting most other trails. One popular 10-mile loop goes to **Sand Point Overlook** for a spectacular view of Monterey

Bay, taking Aptos Creek Fire Road to a side trail nicknamed "The Incline," which climbs 600 feet to the overlook in just

Wakeboarding in Capitola.

one-third of a mile. Most cyclists prefer to ride (or walk) their mountain bikes up it, not down. From the overlook, coast down Hinkley Ridge Trail for six miles back to the parking area. For a longer ride, continue uphill from Sand Point Overlook on a trail known as "The Ladder" for its alternating steep grades and level stretches; it goes about three miles to the summit of Santa Rosalia Mountain, then continues past the park boundary and into the Soquel Demonstration State Forest. Other popular bike trails include the West Ridge Trail, the Olive Springs Trail and the Tractor Trail, the best downhill ride in the park.

Mountain bikers who consider The Forest of Nisene Marks too congested opt for the fire roads and single-tracks of the **Soquel Demonstration State Forest**, a long, narrow 2681-acre expanse of redwoods and mixed hardwoods adjoining the north boundary of Nisene Marks and the east branch of Soquel Creek. It's a good idea to bring a map and compass because the trail network is complex and many trails are unmarked. One recommended 8-mile loop trip, for instance, follows Hihn's Mill Road to the Sulphur Springs Trail, climbs to the Ridge Trail, wanders into The Forest of Nisene Marks State Park, joins the Aptos Creek Fire Road, goes down Buzzard Lagoon Road and returns to the starting point via Highland Road. ~ Highland Way, Laurel; 831-475-8643.

Cyclists who prefer paved-road bike touring will find some intriguing back roads marked with **bike route** signs. They form a continuous route that bypasses the busy freeway stretch of Route 1 south of Santa Cruz. The designated bike route follows Portola Drive to Capitola, then Capitola Road to Soquel, Soquel Drive to Bonita Drive near Rio del Mar, San Andreas Road and West Beach Road to Watsonville, and County Road G12 and Dolan Road to Moss Landing—a distance of 35 miles one-way. For traffic-free biking, try the 9-mile paved **Pajaro River Bike Path**, which starts at the junction of Holohan Road near the airport north of Watsonville and goes south along the edge of town to the river.

You can rent mountain bikes near The Forest of Nisene Marks at **Aptos Bike Trail**. ~ 7556 Soquel Drive, Aptos; 831-688-8650. Touring bike rentals are available at **Family Cycling Center**. ~ 914 41st Avenue, Capitola; 831-475-3883, 800-590-3883; www.familycycling.com.

SURFING

Surfers frequent all the beaches from Santa Cruz south along the bay. In winter, there are good breaks near the jetty, pier and river mouth at **Capitola City Beach**. The protected waters at **New Brighton State Beach** are ideal for beginning surfers. **Manresa State Beach** is one of the most

popular surfing spots on the bay south of Santa Cruz, though shifting sands and seasonal conditions make it unpredictable. **Sunset State Beach** also attracts surfers. The water near the sand bar at **Salinas River State Beach** is a good spot. An even better one is at **Moss Landing State Beach**. There's an outstanding beach break in summer at **Marina State Beach**, but it's hazardous in winter.

Surfboard and wet-suit rentals, as well as lessons, are available at **Schroedel Surfshop** (1054 41st Avenue, Capitola; 831-464-7707; www.schroedel.com) and **O'Neill Surf Shop** (1115 41st Avenue, Capitola; 831-475-4151) as well as Monterey Bay's only women-only surfing outfitter, **Paradise Surf Shop** (3961 Portola Drive, Capitola; 831-462-3880; www.paradisesurf.com).

SPORTFISHING

All the state beaches along the east shore of Monterey Bay offer decent surf fishing for surf perch, sand sole and jack smelt, as do the public piers at **Capitola City Beach** and **Seacliff State Beach**. Local anglers recommend **Moss Landing**, **Salinas River** and **Zmudowski** state beaches.

Capitola Boat and Bait rents 16-foot fishing skiffs as well as fishing gear. ~ Capitola Pier; 831-462-2208.

Deep-sea fishing expeditions in search of salmon and albacore are offered by **Park Place Excursions**. ~ 105 Park Place, Capitola; 831-479-0273, 800-486-1085; www.parkplace excursions.com. Fishing charters are also available at **Tom's Sportfishing**. ~ Harbor District, Moss Landing; 831-633-2564; www.usafishing.com/kahuna.html.

HANG GLIDING & SKYDIVING

Marina State Beach is the region's most popular hang-gliding and paragliding spot, thanks to a combination of usually favorable wind currents and high dunes with a concrete launch ramp at the top. On warm weekends when the wind is right, you'll see dozens of hang gliders circling in search of updrafts that can often carry them five or six miles south along the beach. A U.S. Hang Gliding Association P3 certification is required, though there is no such requirement for another launch ramp three miles down the beach. ~ Route 1, Marina; 831-384-7695. Lessons in hang gliding, paragliding and ultralight flying, as well as tandem flights for beginners, are available right on the beach at **Western Hang Gliders**. ~ Reservation Road, Marina State Beach; 408-384-2622; www. westernhanggliders.org.

In the same area, you can jump out of an airplane and plunge toward the beach at 120 miles an hour with **Skydive Monterey Bay**. It only takes 20 minutes of training to prepare for a tandem freefall jump with an instructor, or you can take a beginners' class in the morning and jump solo the same afternoon. Complete static line and accelerated freefall training programs are also available. You can even arrange for a staff

Sea lions sunning in Monterey Harbor.

Kayaking in Elkhorn Slough.

person to photograph or videotape you during your jump. ~
721 Neeson Road, Suite 1, Marina; 831-384-3483, 888-229-
5867; www.skydivemontereybay.com.

WHALE & WILDLIFE WATCHING

Sanctuary Cruises conducts whale-watching tours
year-round, though outside of the January-through-
March gray whale migration, the high points of the trip are
more likely to be sightings of dolphins, sea otters and sea lions. Their 39-passenger tour boat has underwater viewing
ports; hydrophones let you hear whales and dolphins com-
municating underwater. ~ Harbor District, Moss Landing; 831-
643-0128; www.sanctuarycruises.com.

Another kind of wildlife-watching adventure is offered by
Elkhorn Slough Safari, which takes passengers through **Elkhorn Slough National Estuarine Research Reserve** on a 27-
foot pontoon boat. The tour guide can point out and identify
the myriad species of birds, marine mammals and invertebrates
that thrive in the reserve, which holds the record for the largest
number of bird species ever spotted in a single day anywhere
in North America. ~ Harbor District, Moss Landing; 831-633-
5555; www.elkhornslough.com.

KAYAKING

Kayaking is the best way to explore the maze of channels at **Elkhorn Slough National Estuarine Research Reserve**, one of the few relatively undisturbed coastal wetlands remaining in California. The main channel, lined with cattail marshes and tidal flats, winds inland for nearly seven miles. Expect to see sea otters up close. You'll find rental kayaks near the mouth of the reserve at the **Kayak Connection** (2370 Route 1, Moss Landing; 831-724-5692; www.kayakconnection.com) and **Monterey Bay Kayaks** (2390 Route 1, Moss Landing; 831-373-5357, 800-649-5357; www.montereybaykayaks.com).

RIDING STABLES

You can rent a horse by the hour to ride along the beach at **Monterey Bay Equestrian Center**, located just off Route 1 between Moss Landing and Castroville. ~ 19805 Pesante Road, Salinas; 831-656-0454; www.montereybayeques trian.com.

GOLF

Although the 18-hole **Aptos Seascape Golf Course** lacks the popularity and reputation of the area's big-name courses, the 18-hole, 5813-yard, par-71 course offers challenging, beautifully landscaped, hilly fairways and flawless

greens. Cart rentals are included in the green fee, and club rentals are available. ~ 610 Clubhouse Drive, Aptos; 831-688-3214.

Monterey cypress line the fairways of the **Pajaro Valley Golf Club**, a 6218-yard, par-72 course so close to Elkhorn Slough that you may wonder if you should yell "Fore!" to warn all the birds that perch in the treetops and glide across the sky. Club and cart rentals are available, and the green fees are some of the most

Camping at New Brighton State Beach.

affordable in the Monterey Bay area. ~ 967 Salinas Road, Watsonville; 831-724-3851.

Carved out of a former ranch in the Pajaro Valley as an executive course, **Spring Hills Golf Course** was later expanded to 18 holes. A beautiful setting and a tricky front nine make this 5883-foot, par-71 course a welcome discovery, and green fees are far below the better-known links in the Monterey Bay area. Club and cart rentals are available. ~ 31 Smith Road, Watsonville; 831-724-1404; www.springhillsgc.com.

CAMPING

Set in a quiet wooded area on the bluffs above the shoreline, the **New Brighton State Beach** campground has 112 tent/RV sites that can accommodate motorhomes up to 36 feet long. There are picnic tables, grills and food lockers at each site, but no hookups; the campground has restrooms, pay showers and drinking water. Sites cost $16 to $30 per night. Open year-round. ~ Capitola; 831-464-6330, fax 831-685-6443; reservations 800-444-7275, www.reserveamerica.com.

Nearby **Seacliff State Beach** has a relatively small RV campground so popular that reservations should be made far

in advance. Overlooking the wide, sandy beach and public pier, it's a favorite of fishing enthusiasts but is not suitable for tent camping. There are 26 sites with picnic tables, grills and full hookups for motorhomes up to 40 feet long, as well as an overflow parking area for self-contained campers up to 30 feet long without hookups, tables or grills. The restrooms have pay showers. Sites cost $26 to $39 per night. Open year-round. ~ Capitola; 831-464-6330, fax 831-685-6443; reservations 800-444-7275, www.reserveamerica.com.

Tent campers love **Manresa Uplands Campground** at Manresa State Beach. The 64 walk-in sites, which are not suitable for RVs, are scattered among the pines, and some have views of the bay. The sites are a quarter-mile from the parking area. All sites have picnic tables and grills, and restrooms have pay showers. Drinking water is available. Sites cost $16 to $20 per night. Open April through October. ~ San Andreas Road; 831-761-1795; reservations 800-444-7275, www.reserveamerica.com.

Sunset State Beach has a campground on wooded dune bluffs overlooking the beach, which is strewn with sand dollars and perhaps the prettiest stretch of sand on Monterey Bay. The 90 tent/RV sites, which can accommodate vehicles up to 31 feet long, have picnic tables, grills and food lockers. There are restrooms with pay showers, and you can buy firewood at the campground entrance. Sites cost $16 to $20 per night. Open year-round. ~ San Andreas Road; 831-763-7063, fax 831-763-7120; reservations 800-444-7275, www.reserveamerica.com.

Unlike most area RV parks, **Pinto Lake Park** north of Watsonville has no swimming pool, showers, laundry or picnic tables. Not even a video game room. It allows no tent camping and no swimming in the lake, but it does have water, sewer, electric and cable TV hookups for motorhomes up to 50 feet long, as well as local ISP access for laptop computers. Its vast lawn fronts a peaceful, undeveloped lake surrounded by pines. Rowboats and pedal boats are available for rent, and there's a launch ramp for nonmotorized craft. The lake is stocked with trout every two weeks. Reservations are advisable on weekends, though usually unnecessary during the week. Sites cost $25 per night. Open year-round. ~ 451 Green Valley Road, Watsonville; 831-722-8129; www.pintolake.com, e-mail camp ing@pintolake.com.

lodging

In Capitola, you'll find units with full kitchens and ocean views at the **Harbor Lights Motel**. The stucco motor inn is small—just ten rooms— and comfortably furnished, but its best feature is the location just steps away from the beach. ~ 5000 Cliff Drive, Capitola; 831-476-0505, fax 831-476-0235. MODERATE TO ULTRA-DELUXE.

The **Inn at Depot Hill** offers luxury accommodations with an international flair. Each of the 12 guest rooms is decorated in a different exotic motif; choose from "Paris," "Portofino" or "Côte d'Azur," among others. All rooms boast fireplaces, and most have hot tubs and patios. Guests are welcomed with

hors d'oeuvres and wine and greeted the next morning with a full gourmet breakfast. ~ 250 Monterey Avenue, Capitola; 831-462-3376, 800-572-2632, fax 831-462-3697; www.innatdepot hill.com, e-mail lodging@innatdepothill.com. ULTRA-DELUXE.

In nearby Soquel, guests sleep warm and cozy at the **Blue Spruce Inn**, where most of the six rooms—three in the main house and three more in the garden area—have fireplaces and jacuzzis. One even has a private garden with a hot tub. Afternoon wine and a full breakfast are included in the rate. ~ 2815 South Main Street, Soquel; 831-464-1137, 800-559-1137, fax 831-475-0608; www.bluespruce.com, e-mail vtjecha@blue spruce.com. DELUXE.

A stately redwood Arts-and-Crafts-style mansion built by a wine grape grower in 1895, **Historic Sand Rock Farm** stands on a ten-acre estate where tall trees, a shade garden and a rose garden with an old millstone fountain make for a peaceful retreat. The five guest rooms are individually and graciously decorated and have garden views; several feature jacuzzis. One of the innkeepers, a well-known San Francisco chef who discovered the mansion while exploring the area's small wineries, prepares seasonal gourmet breakfasts. She also serves other gourmet meals by reservation only, teaches cooking classes and guides tours of local farmers' markets and wineries. ~ 6901 Freedom Road, Aptos; 831-688-8005, fax 831-688-8025; www.sandrock farm.com, e-mail staff@sandrockfarm.com. ULTRA-DELUXE.

California's Oldest Inn

The oldest continuously operating inn in the state of California, the **Bayview Hotel Bed and Breakfast** was built in 1878—but not at its current location. The stately mansard-roofed New Orleans–style hotel used to stand across from the Aptos train station and marked the center of town until 1942, when it was jacked up and relocated to its present garden setting. During its restoration in the 1990s, walls were removed to transform the original 28 units to 12 spacious rooms and suites lavishly redecorated in Victorian-era splendor. Some, but not all, rooms have private baths, and some have fireplaces. A continental breakfast and afternoon fruit and sherry are included in the room rate. ~ 8041 Soquel Drive, Aptos; 831-688-8654, 800-422-9843; www.bayviewhotel.com, e-mail lodging@bayviewhotel.com. DELUXE.

Vacation home at Pajaro Dunes.

Also in Aptos, **Seascape Resort** has 285 studio suites and one- and two-bedroom villas overlooking the beach and bay from a bluff near Aptos Seascape Golf Course, where guests have priority in reserving tee times. All guest units have fully equipped kitchens or kitchenettes as well as fireplaces and private balconies and king- or queen-size beds. Gourmet room service is available. The three-story complex has three outdoor swimming pools. In summer, a Kids Club program sets parents free by offering activities, field trips and nightly movies for children ages 5 to 12. ~ 1 Seascape Resort Drive, Aptos; 831-688-6800, 800-929-7727, fax 831-685-0615; www.seascape resort.com, e-mail tani@seascaperesort.com. ULTRA-DELUXE.

If a lively beach resort scene fits your travel style, you'll find 130 condos, townhouses and beach houses at **Pajaro Dunes Vacation and Conference Center**. The location, at the south end of Sunset State Beach, is one of the prettiest spots on the bay shore and has been a popular getaway spot since the 1930s, when it was known as Palm Beach (although there are no palm trees here, just seashells and spectacular sunsets). Owned as vacation-and-income properties, the condos and houses are individually decorated; all have kitchens, fireplaces, decks and barbecues. Though the rates are steep, a three-bedroom house can be a bargain for a large family or group traveling together. Resort facilities include 19 tennis courts. ~ 2661 Beach Road, Watsonville; 831-722-9201, 800-564-1771; www.pajarodunes.com, e-mail info@pajarodunes.com. ULTRA-DELUXE.

The California Coastal Act of 1976 imposed environmental requirements and hearing procedures so tough that not a single resort or subdivision development was built anywhere on the state's coastline for more than 20 years—until **Marina Dunes Resort** won approval to build on the unsightly site of an old sand quarry while funding a dunes restoration project and habitat preservation for the endangered snowy plover, Smith's blue butterfly and California legless lizard, all of which live on the resort's land. Guest accommodations are in luxurious bungalows scattered among 19 acres of secluded sand dunes. They are sumptuously decorated in earth tones, and all have ocean or dune views, fireplaces and balconies or patios. The recreation trail that starts at the main lodge offers some of the best bay views around. A full-service spa pampers guests with aromatherapy and hot porcelain massages. There's a restaurant and tapas bar decorated in Old West style on the premises, and limited room service is available. ~ 3295 Dunes Drive, Marina; 831-883-9478, 877-944-3863, fax 831-883-9477; www.marinadunes.com, e-mail info@marinadunes.com. ULTRA-DELUXE.

• •

Lunch with the Steinbecks

In Salinas, the **Steinbeck House Restaurant**—the big Victorian-style residence where author John Steinbeck was born and raised—funds the nonprofit group dedicated to its restoration. Open only for lunch, the restaurant serves a fixed-price meal, including appetizers, entrée and beverage (dessert costs extra), that changes weekly and highlights produce grown in the Salinas Valley. Reservations are essential and should be made a week in advance. Closed Sundays. ~ 132 Central Avenue, Salinas; 831-424-2735; www.infopoint.com/mry/orgs/steinbeck.

• •

Considered the finest Santa Cruz area restaurant ever since it opened in 1947, the **Shadowbrook Restaurant** has a creekside setting wrapped in tall coastal 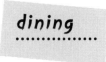 forest. A pathway fringed with giant ferns sets the stage for the eight dining and lounge areas in the vast multi-level interior, where potted plants, stone fireplaces and elegant table settings set the ambience. Vines clamber up the walls of some rooms, and in one a living tree grows through the floor and ceiling. Besides the traditional prime rib, seafood and pasta menu, the restaurant has a full schedule of weekly dinner specials, Sunday champagne brunch and family-night dinner, and Winemaker Wednesdays, featuring a different Santa Cruz Mountains vintner weekly. No lunch on Saturday. ~ 1750 Wharf Road, Capitola; 831-475-1511; www.shadowbrook-capitola.com, e-mail office@shadow brook-capitola.com. MODERATE TO DELUXE.

Dharmaland offers natural vegetarian cuisine, with specialties that include a portobello and artichoke sub, a gardener's salad heaped with lettuce, carrots, cucumbers, beets, tomatoes, sprouts and seeds, and Greek pasta with garlic, sun-dried tomatoes, spinach and Kalamata olives. There are also vegetarian Thai and Mexican selections and four different kinds of veggie burgers. ~ 4250 Capitola Road, Capitola; 831-462-1717, fax 831-464-8638; www.dharmaland.com. BUDGET.

A Capitola institution, **Gayle's Bakery & Rosticceria** started in 1978 as an 800-square-foot bakery and gradually expanded to become a 10,000-square-foot fast-food emporium that employs 115 people and publishes its own cookbooks. A huge menu offers more than a dozen salads, hot and cold roasted meats, pastas, casseroles and changing blue-plate specials, making Gayle's a great place to pick up picnic fixings. They take pride in the fact that everything they serve is made from scratch—even the mayonnaise. ~ 504 Bay Avenue, Capitola; 831-462-1200; www.gaylesbakery.com. BUDGET.

Bittersweet Express, a small indoor/outdoor café, is a local morningtime favorite for breakfast burritos, gourmet coffee and pastries. For lunch and beach picnics, there are sandwiches, salads and hot deli items. Dinner features an assortment of eat-there-or-take-out entrées from barbecued ribs to vegetarian lasagna, and each day brings a different fixed-price "Don't Feel Like Cooking" special. ~ 787 Rio Del Mar Boulevard, Aptos; 831-662-9899; www.bittersweetexpress.com. BUDGET TO MODERATE.

For a touch of the tropics, try **Palapa's Restaurant y Cantina**, so authentic that you could imagine yourself in Mazatlán or Playa del Carmen if it weren't for occasional fog and the absence of palm trees. Seafood and sauces of coastal Mexico

The Whole Enchilada.

are prepared *a la cocina fresca.* There's a gorgeous view of Monterey Bay. ~ 21 Seascape Village, Aptos; 831-662-9000. BUDGET TO MODERATE.

In Moss Landing, **Phil's Fish Market & Eatery** features fish and shellfish fresh off the boat. The decor inside is rather plain, while the heated outdoor seating area places you amid all the local color of the old-fashioned fishing village. Along with familiar seafood restaurant fare such as salmon, swordfish, mahimahi and albacore, the menu lists unusual choices such as skate wings, leopard shark steaks and California sea bass, as well as crabs, oysters and octopus. ~ 7600 Sandholdt Road, Moss Landing; 831-633-2152, fax 831-633-8611; www.phils fishmarket.com. MODERATE.

Some folks say **The Whole Enchilada** is the best Mexican restaurant in Monterey County. Its chef uses locally grown produce such as chiles and Castroville artichokes, along with fresh-caught fish, prawns and shellfish, to present new twists on old favorites, such as its namesake "whole enchilada" entrée—*huachinango* (red snapper) wrapped in fresh corn tortillas and topped with chile salsa and Monterey Jack cheese. ~ Route 1 at Moss Landing Road, Moss Landing; 831-633-5398. BUDGET TO MODERATE.

On weekend nights only, the **Shadowbrook Restaurant** presents mellow live music in its sumptuous, gently lit lounge. ~ 1750 Wharf Road, Capitola; 831-475-1511; www.shadowbrook-capitola.com.

nightlife
• • • • • • • • • • • • • • •

Severino's at the Best Western Seacliff Inn in Aptos claims that its two-hour-long weeknight happy hour is the most popular happy hour in the Santa Cruz area, perhaps because of the free hors d'oeuvres and live music. ~ 7500 Old Dominion Court, Aptos; 831-688-7300; www.seacliffinn.com.

For something a little livelier, try the **Aptos Club**, which showcases San Francisco Bay Area alternative rock and hip-hop acts. Cover. ~ 7941 Soquel Drive, Aptos; 831-688-9888.

The self-consciously anglophilic **Britannia Arms Pub** offers dart boards, a big-screen TV showing soccer games, a three-hour happy hour and live music. The "pub grub" menu features fish-and-chips, steak-and-kidney pie and bangers and mash, as well as a small store that sells British foodstuffs (perfect for picnicking on really foggy days). ~ 8017 Soquel Drive, Aptos; 831-688-1233; www.britanniaarms.com.

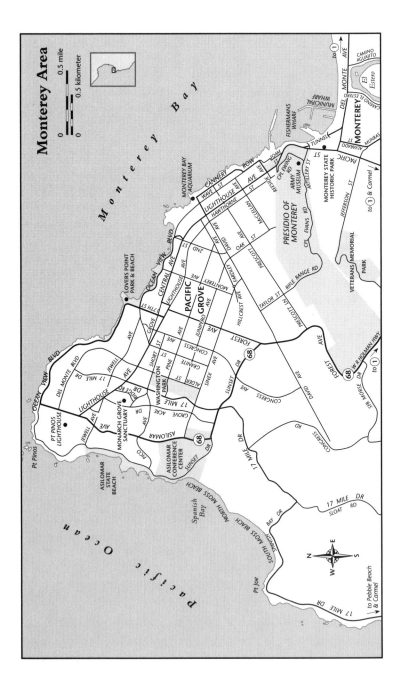

Monterey Area

0 0.5 mile
0 0.5 kilometer

Monterey Bay

MONTEREY BAY AQUARIUM

LOVERS POINT PARK & BEACH

CANNERY ROW

Monterey Bay

OCEAN VIEW BLVD

CENTRAL AVE

PACIFIC GROVE

LIGHTHOUSE AVE

WAVE ST

LIGHTHOUSE AVE

HAWTHORNE

2ND ST

DAVID AVE

PRESCOTT AVE

MONTEREY AVE

HILLCREST AVE

FOUNTAIN AVE

MCCLELLAN AVE

PIKO AVE

SLOAN ST

CANNERY ROW

CPL EWING RD

ARMY MUSEUM

ARTILLERY ST

PRESIDIO OF MONTEREY

CPL EVANS RD

RIFLE RANGE RD

TAYLOR ST

PRESCOTT AVE

FOREST AVE

FOREST AVE

JUNIPERO AVE

CONGRESS AVE

PINE AVE

GRANITE ST

ALDER ST

PINES AVE

SUNSET DR

SHORT ST

GROVE ST

FOUNTAIN AVE

DEL MONTE BLVD

ASILOMAR AVE

OCEAN VIEW BLVD

LIGHTHOUSE AVE

POWELL AVE

JEWELL AVE

17 MILE DR

PINE AVE

PRICE RD

WASHINGTON PARK

ACRE AVE

GROVE ACRE AVE

CONGRESS AVE

PT PINOS LIGHTHOUSE

Pt Pinos

MONARCH GROVE SANCTUARY

17 MILE DR

ASILOMAR CONFERENCE CENTER

PICO AVE

ASILOMAR STATE BEACH

SUNSET DR

68

68

68

Spanish Bay

NORTH MOSS BEACH

SOUTH MOSS BEACH

SPANISH BAY DR

17 MILE DR

Pt Joe

DAVID AVE

CONGRESS RD

SEB MORSE DR

17 MILE DR

DAVID AVE

FOREST AVE

W H HOLMAN HWY

to 1

68

17 MILE DR

SLOAT RD

to Pebble Beach & Carmel

Pacific Ocean

N W E S

TUNNEL

FISHERMANS WHARF

MUNICIPAL WHARF

MONTEREY

DEL MONTE AVE

CAMINO AGUAJITO

CAMINO EL ESTERO

El Estero

JEFFERSON ST

MONTEREY STATE HISTORIC PARK

PACIFIC ST

ALVARADO ST

MUNRAS AVE

VETERANS MEMORIAL PARK

FOREST AVE

to 1 & Carmel

4

Monterey

The adjoining towns of Monterey (pop. 32,000) and Pacific Grove (pop. 16,000) extend along the north coast of the Monterey Peninsula. Together, the two communities are home to the majority of Monterey Bay area residents. Even so, nature is a constant presence in the Monterey area, from the beaches, tidepools and rocky points along the coast to the rugged pine-forested ridges in the interior. Busy Route 1 slices across the landward side of the peninsula, separating this magical place from the more mundane farming valleys to the east and making it feel more like an island hideaway than an appendage of mainland California.

Monterey wears its history on its sleeve—and what a history it is! Though other parts of the Monterey Bay area invite active visitors to explore the natural world in its

many manifestations, Monterey entices them to hike or bike right in the middle of the city and discover old adobe mansions dating back to Spanish colonial times. There are buildings that housed the U.S. Consulate to Mexican California, the original state capital where the California Constitution was signed and the state's first theater. There are lavish gardens edged with whalebones from the 19th century, when whale oil was Monterey's main stock in trade, and canning factories from the early 20th century, when whales were replaced by sardines. The spirit of Nobel Prize–winning author John Steinbeck pervades the city of Monterey in much the same way that neighboring Pacific Grove celebrates its monarch butterflies. It all adds up to a unique local character that visitors flock to experience for themselves.

Add a full complement of water sports, from surf fishing right off the old fishing fleet wharfs and scuba diving directly from the beach to kayaking along the scenic, sheltered shoreline. Throw in some of California's best golf, including Scottish-style links, the oldest course in the West and a pair of courses that have been known to baffle even the pros. End the day at a fine restaurant and exceptional lodging and you have all the elements for a vacation getaway that blends adventure, romance and a touch of luxury.

sightseeing

Of the four Monterey exits from Route 1, the best one to take as a visitor is the Pacific Street/Munras Avenue exit. Pacific Street take you directly to most of the sightseeing attractions in town, and Munras is where you'll find moderately priced motels.

Monterey is best explored on foot. The most convenient public parking lot is the one at **Fisherman's Wharf**. The wharf itself, like San Francisco's wharf of the same name, has become the kind of place that tourism developers seem to think visitors expect a fishermen's wharf to be, with street performers, art galleries, curio shops and glass-bottom boat and whale-watching tour operators galore. Sure, there is still a fishmonger here and there with the catch of the day, mouths agape, laid out on ice, but they are basically part of the show, too. Few visitors to Fisherman's Wharf buy fish as souvenirs, and at the end of the day most of them wind up in the kitchens of the seafood restaurants that abound up and down the wharf. It's hard to imagine one of the whalers and salmon and sardine fishermen of yore slogging along the wharf or cleaning fish and tossing the guts overboard for the gulls and pelicans. The boutique and gallery owners would never stand for it.

The last vestiges of the commercial fishing industry can be found several blocks east, past the municipal marina, at **Municipal Wharf #2**. Fishing boats rock and bump against the used tires that protect the wharf, while elsewhere along its length shore fishermen put their luck to the test. Sea lions, too, vie for the fish that swim among the moorings, and seabirds eye anglers with eager anticipation as they clean their catch. There are also defunct refrigerated warehouses and factorylike fish companies—a few of them still operating—with creaky old cranes, conveyor belts and forklifts, cast-off packing crates and all the detritus of a once-thriving industry. The smells of the sea and its bounty mingle, helping to preserve the fishy "charm" that Fisherman's Wharf has lost. ~ Located at the foot of Figueroa Street.

The centuries of Monterey are enshrined in its historic architecture, the best-preserved examples of which line the two-mile **Path of History**. Guided walking tours run hourly from 10 a.m. to 3 p.m., starting from the Stanton Center Maritime Museum. The various tours throughout the day are different, and each includes walk-throughs of historic buildings that may include the Cooper-Molera Adobe, the Larkin House or Casa Soberanes as well as the maritime museum. Fee. ~ For a current tour schedule, call 831-649-7118.

It's easy to explore the Path of History on your own by following the markers set in the sidewalks and reading the plaques

Celebrating the annual Monterey City Birthday.

Custom House.

in front of the buildings; a walking tour brochure is available at most stops along the route. Many of the historic structures are owned by the state of California as part of **Monterey State Historic Park**, while others are private residences or B&Bs. Some, but not all, are open to the public—sometimes for limited hours. The same fee you'd pay for the guided tour will buy a pass admitting you to all the public buildings. ~ 831-649-7118.

Although you can join the Path of History at any point along the route, the natural place to start is the **Custom House**, located across from Fisherman's Wharf. The only building still standing in California that was built by the Mexican government, it housed the agency that collected tariffs on cargo arriving in Monterey by ship. Constructed in 1822 (the same year Mexico won its independence from Spain) on the site of a demolished Spanish colonial government building, it presided over the port until 1846, the year territorial California was ceded to the United States. Today the stone-and-adobe Custom House serves as a museum exhibiting the kinds of goods

GHOSTS OF CHRISTMAS PAST

Monterey State Historic Park celebrates the holiday season with an annual **Christmas in the Adobes** tour. Luminaria candles line the sidewalks and rooflines of the Path of History, and volunteers dressed in period costumes welcome you into colonial homes in the historic district for steaming hot cider and cookies. For information and tour reservations, call 831-649-7118.

that would have arrived as cargo in Mexican times. ~ 1 Custom House Plaza.

Across Custom House Plaza, **Pacific House** dates back to 1835 and was built by James McKinley, a Scottish immigrant, as a hotel and saloon. Over the years, the long two-story building served a variety of sometimes contradictory functions. For instance, in the 1850s it housed the county courtroom and clerk's office alongside the seaport's most notorious sailors' bar. Bear fights were staged in the central courtyard, now called the "Memory Garden." Today it houses a historical museum downstairs and the Monterey Museum of the American Indian upstairs. ~ 10 Custom House Plaza; 831-649-7118.

Just behind Pacific House stands the small two-story adobe **Casa de Oro**. Despite its Spanish name, which translates as House of Gold, it was built by the U.S. Army in 1849 as barracks and later used as a hospital for sailors before Joseph Boston bought it and converted it into a general store. Its name comes from a time when it served as a gold-dust exchange and assay office. Today it operates once again as the Joseph Boston Store, an old-fashioned shop that sells historic curios, and is owned by the Monterey Historic Garden League. Closed Mondays through Wednesdays. ~ Olivier and Scott streets; 831-649-3364.

Diagonally across Olivier Street stands the **First Brick House**—the first in California, or so they say. It was built by

Pacific House.

••
American Monterey
When California became a state, Monterey remained its capital for only a short time. The state constitutional convention was held there, but the Gold Rush had already shifted economic power northward, so the capital was soon moved to Sacramento. In the years that followed, Monterey prospered as a whaling and fishing port. Meanwhile Methodist settlers established nearby Pacific Grove as a religious retreat and built the first resort hotel on Monterey Bay, attracting 17,000 tourists a year—a phenomenal number for that time.

In the 20th century, electricity caused the demand for whale oil to drop sharply, and soon the sea's largest creatures were replaced by some of the smallest—sardines—as Monterey's economic mainstay. The sardine catch, too, later declined as the fish became scarce. Fortunately, tourists have only grown more abundant and have served as the mainstay of Monterey's economy for the past 60 years.
••

a Virginia businessman in 1947, but he abandoned it to seek his fortune in the gold fields before it was completed; the house was auctioned off along with a pile of 60,000 red bricks for $1000 cash. ~ 351 Decatur Street.

Next door, the **Whaling Station** dates back to 1855, when it was built as a boarding house for Portuguese whalers. Its name comes from rumors that its second-floor veranda was used to spot whales. You can still see whalebones embedded in the sidewalk. Behind the building is a beautiful garden, made available for weddings by the Junior League, which owns the property. ~ 391 Decatur Street; 831-375-5356.

A block up Pacific Street, **California's First Theatre** was built in 1844 as a boarding house for sailors with an attached saloon, then converted to a theater in 1847. Today it continues to present authentic 19th-century melodramas, performed by America's oldest continually operating theater troupe. ~ Pacific Street at Scott Street; 831-375-4916.

Across the street, the Victorian-style woodframe **Perry House** was constructed by a whaling captain in the 1880s. It now serves as the headquarters for the Monterey History and Art Association and displays the association's Historic Fashion Collection of clothing from the late 18th century to the present day. ~ 201 Scott Street; 831-375-9182.

Follow Pacific Street south for two blocks to **Casa Soberanes**, a key sight on guided Path of History tours. Built by a Mexican don around 1830, the tile-roofed "House with the Blue Gate" stands on a hillside secluded behind a tall hedge. The house is a showplace of antique furnishings and decorative items from around the world, reflecting the international trade that made Monterey a busy seaport in the 19th century.

Half-hour tours are available at 10 a.m., 3 p.m. and 4 p.m. Equally enchanting are the terraced gardens edged with whalebones, shells and century-old wine bottles. Admission. ~ 336 Pacific Street; 831-649-7118.

Casa Soberanes.

Continuing another block up Pacific Street will bring you to the two-story adobe **Merritt House**, built by a Spanish don in 1774 and later given a wood facade when it became the residence of Monterey's first Anglo county judge, one of the new wave of "founding fathers" who took control of the area when it became U.S. territory. Today the Merritt House operates as a B&B (see "Lodging" below). The lobby area is open to the public. ~ 386 Pacific Street; 831-646-9686, 800-541-5599, fax 831-646-5392; www.merritthouse inn.com, e-mail info@merritthouseinn.com.

Another block up Pacific Street, **Casa Serrano**'s classically utilitarian architecture resembles at first glance a run-of-the-mill suburban house you'd expect to find in all-American suburbia. In fact, the adobe house remains almost unchanged since it was built by a Mexican don in 1845. It served as a schoolhouse for a time and is now a private residence again. ~ 412 Pacific Street.

Colton Hall.

Turn right following the Path of History markers and go one block west, then turn left on Pierce Street, where you'll find the **Lara-Soto Adobe**. Originally built in 1851 by a member of the Soberanes family, this narrow single-story house changed hands several times before it was abandoned and left to deteriorate. It was resurrected and restored in 1940 by local artist Josephine Blanch. She then sold it in 1944 to John Steinbeck, who lived there while completing *Cannery Row*. It continues to be a private residence. ~ Pierce and Jefferson streets.

In the next block up Pierce Street, several noteworthy buildings front on shady, parklike **Friendly Plaza**. The **Monterey Peninsula Museum of Art**, one of the few points of interest in the area that is not in a historic building, showcases works by area artists, both past and present. Closed Mondays and Tuesdays. Admission. ~ 559 Pacific Street; 831-372-5477; www. montereyart.org, e-mail mtryart@mbay.net.

Originally built as a school and meeting hall, **Colton Hall** is venerated as the site of the 1849 constitutional convention that resulted in California's statehood the following year. The second floor has been restored and contains displays about the convention, which is reenacted each year on October 13. The ground floor is occupied by municipal offices. ~ Pacific Street between Jefferson and Madison streets; 831-646-5640. Directly behind Colton Hall, the **Old Jail** housed prisoners whose hard-labor sentences went into building Colton Hall.

Casa Gutierrez was built in 1836 by a former Mexican governor of California. Now home to a small historical museum and cultural center, it is notable for its peaceful courtyard with fountain and portico. Admission. ~ Calle Principal near Madison Street.

On the same block is the **Larkin House**, one of the most historically significant buildings on the Path of History tour. Built in 1834 by immigrant Yankee merchant Thomas Larkin, the two-story house with a wrap-

Rose room in the Larkin House.

around veranda became a consulate when Larkin was appointed the first U.S. Consul to Mexican California in 1843. It then served as the headquarters for the military governor of California when the territory was ceded to the United States. It's now a museum filled with 19th-century furnishings and

Larkin House.

Cooper-Molera Adobe.

household goods. Daily tours are available. Admission. ~ 510 Calle Principal; 831-649-7118; e-mail mshpl@mbay.net.

Next door, a crumbling adobe facade marks the **Sherman Headquarters**, which was built in 1834 as part of the Larkin estate and later used by William T. Sherman, the general remembered for his devastating march through Georgia during the Civil War. Of course, when Sherman did his tour of duty in Monterey as an adjutant to the military governor from 1847 to 1849, he was only a lieutenant.

Take a right on Jefferson Street and then a quick right on Polk Street to find a cluster of other historic homes from the Mexican period. Two-story **Casa Amesti**, built in 1825, is considered one of Monterey's best examples of post-colonial adobe architecture. It's now a private club. ~ 516 Polk Street.

The **Cooper-Molera Adobe**, built by sea captain John Roger Cooper, a half-brother of Thomas Larkin who succeeded Larkin as U.S. Consul to California, is noteworthy in that it combines two large homes—a 1830s adobe and a two-story Victorian-era home. Also on the two-and-a-half-acre estate are two barns, a garden and a state park visitors center. Guided tours are given three times daily. Admission. ~ 525 Polk Street; 831-649-7118; e-mail mshpl@mbay.net.

At the corner of Polk and Hartnell streets, the **Gabriel Adobe** was built in 1836 by a Mexican *alcalde* (mayor) and is one of the oldest surviving houses in Monterey. It was later used as a courthouse under both Mexican and U.S. rule. Across the street, the big pink **Stokes Adobe** was built in 1840 by a physician who became Monterey's first Anglo mayor.

Backtrack down Polk Street for one block to a five-way intersection and turn right on Pearl Street, then right again on Houston Street, to find the **Stevenson House**. Originally built

Stevenson House.

in 1840, the "house" was actually the French Hotel, where author Robert Louis Stevenson stayed for several months in 1879 while visiting Monterey for the purpose of courting his future wife, Fanny Osbourne. It's now owned by the state of California, and several rooms have been opened to the public to display period hotel furnishings and Stevenson exhibits. ~ 530 Houston Street.

Continue up Houston Street and turn left on Webster Street. At the corner of Webster and Abrego streets, the **Casa Pacheco** was built in 1840. When the building was restored in 1929, the main entrance was moved from the Webster side to the Abrego side, and the wrought-iron balconies that once defined the old adobe house were replaced by a wooden false veranda.

••
Adobe Abodes

Most houses built in Monterey during the Spanish colonial and Mexican eras were made of adobe, a type of sunbaked clay-and-straw brick. Adobe construction originated in the deserts of North Africa and the Middle East and was brought to Spain by the Moors (Moroccans) who ruled the Iberian Peninsula during the Middle Ages. It was not particularly well-suited to withstand the fog and damp winters of California's central coast, since the main drawback of adobe is that it gradually melts back into mud when exposed to moisture. In colonial times, plastering the exteriors of adobe houses with fresh protective layers of clay was a constant chore. Today Monterey's historic adobe houses are covered with concrete stucco to keep the dampness out, then whitewashed.
••

Turn right on Abrego at Casa Pacheco, then left on the next corner to Church Street, where the ornate sandstone facade and heavy wooden doors of the **Royal Presidio Chapel** stand as a graceful reminder of Spanish colonial Monterey. The single massive, square bell tower that stands to one side of the chapel makes it look curiously unbalanced. The chapel was part of the Mission of San Carlos de Borromeo de Monterey, built in 1770 by Father Junipero Serra. Soon after, the mission was relocated to a new church at the mouth of the Carmel River on the other side of the peninsula, and this church was turned over to the Spanish Army. In 1789, fire damaged the former mission church. The portion still standing—the chapel and one bell tower—was rebuilt and rededicated in 1795. It has been used continuously ever since. Inside the long, narrow chapel hangs a series of dark, crackled oil paintings depicting biblical events as imagined by 18th-century Spanish church artists. A self-guided tour brochure is available. ~ 550 Church Street.

Ship model at the Maritime Museum of Monterey.

Returning to the starting point on the Path of History means retracing your route for four blocks, past the Stevenson House, to turn left on Pearl Street and then take the next right onto Tyler Street. Here you'll find the **Casa Estrada**, a three-story adobe mansion that was one of the tallest buildings in Monterey when it was built in 1823. During its varied history it has served as a hotel, an office building and a bank.

Beyond Casa Estrada, turn left on Bonifacio Place and then right on Alvarado Street. Walking three blocks down Alvarado will bring you back to the waterfront at the **Maritime Museum of Monterey**, where your tour ends among model ships, a World War II exhibit and a rotating two-story-tall lighthouse lens. Closed Monday. Admission. ~ 5 Custom House Plaza; 831-372-2608; www.mntmh.org/maritime.htm.

OPPOSITE: Maritime Museum of Monterey's Frensel Lens.

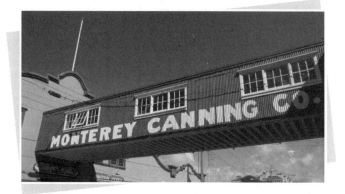

West of Fisherman's Wharf and the historic district lies the **Presidio of Monterey**, a fortified U.S. Army base on a knoll overlooking the town and the bay. The original Spanish presidio, established beside the mission church that is now the Royal Presidio Chapel, was gradually moved to this location for its commanding view of the waterfront. An **Army Museum** at Artillery Street and Ewing Road recounts the presidio's long history under three flags. Nearby, several monuments recall key events in Monterey's past. The **Serra Monument** at Pacific and Artillery streets marks the spot where Father Junipero Serra, the Franciscan priest who established many of California's mission churches, held the first Catholic mass in California. The inconspicuous **Bouchard Monument** is dedicated to the French pirate Hippolyte de Bouchard, who seized Monterey in 1818 and claimed the peninsula in the name of Argentina, holding the presidio for a month before supplies dwindled and he and his crew left in search of new ports to loot. Behind the Army Museum, the **Sloat Monument** commemorates the bloodless takeover of California by U.S. troops in 1846. Nearby, five cannons are almost all that remains of the ruined **Fort Mervine**, built by the U.S. Army in 1846. All but one of the cannons were installed during the U.S. Civil War. After the war, the presidio was abandoned until the 20th century. Today it is the last former Spanish presidio in California that is still used as a military base. It is open to the public, though gate security has been tightened due to terrorism fears. ~

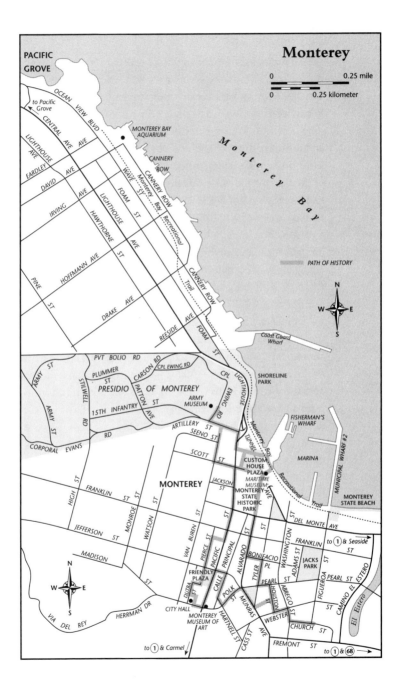

Monterey

PACIFIC GROVE

to Pacific Grove

OCEAN VIEW BLVD

CENTRAL AVE

LIGHTHOUSE AVE

EARDLEY AVE

DAVID AVE

IRVING AVE

PINE ST

HOFFMANN AVE

HAWTHORNE AVE

LIGHTHOUSE AVE

FOAM ST

WAVE ST

Monterey Bay Recreational

DRAKE AVE

REESIDE AVE

FOAM ST

MONTEREY BAY AQUARIUM

CANNERY ROW

CANNERY ROW

Trail

0   0.25 mile
0   0.25 kilometer

Monterey Bay

PATH OF HISTORY

N
W   E
S

Coast Guard Wharf

PVT BOLIO RD

PLUMMER ST

ARMY ST

STILWELL RD

CARSON RD

CPL EWING RD

PRESIDIO OF MONTEREY

PATTON AVE

15TH INFANTRY AVE

ARMY ST

CORPORAL EVANS RD

CPL LIGHTHOUSE

CPL EWING RD

ARMY MUSEUM

SHORELINE PARK

ARTILLERY ST

SEENO ST

SCOTT ST

Monterey Bay

TUNNEL

FISHERMAN'S WHARF

MARINA

MUNICIPAL WHARF #2

MONTEREY STATE BEACH

HIGH ST

FRANKLIN ST

MONROE ST

WATSON ST

MONTEREY

JACKSON ST

CUSTOM HOUSE PLAZA

MARITIME MUSEUM

MONTEREY STATE HISTORIC PARK

MONTEREY AVE

Recreational Trail

JEFFERSON ST

MADISON ST

VAN BUREN ST

PIERCE ST

PACIFIC ST

CALLE PRINCIPAL

ALVARADO ST

BONIFACIO PL

TYLER ST

POLK ST

WASHINGTON ST

ADAMS ST

FRANKLIN ST

DEL MONTE AVE

to ① & Seaside

JACKS PARK

FIGUEROA ST

PEARL ST

CAMINO EL ESTERO

EL Estero

FRIENDLY PLAZA

CITY HALL

MONTEREY MUSEUM OF ART

VIA DEL REY

HERRMAN DR

DUTRA ST

MUNRAS AVE

PEARL ST

HOUSTON ST

ABREGO ST

WEBSTER ST

CHURCH ST

CASS ST

HARTNELL ST

to ① & Carmel

FREMONT ST

to ① & ㊸

Pacific and Artillery streets; 831-242-5555, fax 831-242-5464; www.dli-army.mil.

Continue west from the presidio on Foam Street, then turn right to reach Monterey's other historic district, **Cannery Row**. The same sort of gentrification that transformed Fisherman's Wharf also invaded this five-block strip of former sardine-canning factories. In its heyday, Cannery Row had 30 canneries and a fleet of 100 fishing boats and employed 4000 workers. Most of the old sardine-canning plants that blocked the view of the ocean from what was then called Ocean View Avenue had already shut down by 1945, when John Steinbeck's novel *Cannery Row* was published. Although Steinbeck himself was a persona non grata in Monterey during his lifetime, his book brought such fame to the district that in 1953 the city officially changed the street name from Ocean View Avenue to Cannery Row. On his final visit, Steinbeck observed that "They fish for tourists now."

Steinbeck buffs can still see the weatherbeaten exterior of the old wooden building that housed **"Doc's Western Biological Laboratory"**—actually Dr. Ed Ricketts' Pacific Biological Laboratory. ~ 800 Cannery Row. Almost directly across the street, **Kalisa's La Ida Café** has been transformed from a bar into an ice cream parlor but still retains its tumble-down look from the old days. ~ 851 Cannery Row; 831-644-9316. *Cannery Row*'s other major settings, the Palace Flophouse (which really existed) and the Bear Flag Restaurant (actually a brothel called the Lone Star Café) were located within two blocks, but time has changed them beyond recognition. Many of the old sardine warehouses have become indoor malls filled with art galleries, boutiques, curio shops and a plethora of restaurants. If fictional characters had graves, Mack and the boys would no doubt be rolling over in theirs.

The major attraction of modern-day Cannery Row, the **Monterey Bay Aquarium** is one of the best public aquariums anywhere. The galleries replicate Monterey Bay's undersea environments, from shallow tidepools to open ocean. The centerpiece, a million-gallon Outer Bay tank, can

Opposite: Monterey Bay Aquarium.

•••••••••••••••••••••••••••••

JUST FOR KIDS

One of the old sardine-factory warehouses along Cannery Row now houses the **Edgewater Family Fun Center**, a state-of-the-art video-game arcade that also has bike rentals, mini golf and a 1905 hand-carved carousel. ~ 640 Wave Street, Monterey; 831-649-1899; www.monterey fun.com.

•••••••••••••••••••••••••••••

be viewed from two levels and contains sharks, tuna and sea turtles. The unique three-story Kelp Forest exhibit offers a close-up look at the inhabitants of the sheltering aquatic jungle off the coastline of the bay. The Mysteries of the Deep tank is the largest exhibit of living deep-sea creatures ever created and includes a live video feed from the depths of the bay's undersea canyon. The Splash Zone touch tank offers kids a chance to feel starfish and bat rays. Perhaps the most striking exhibit in the aquarium is Jellies: Living Art, a fascinating look at various species of delicate jellyfish, side-lit to make the nearly transparent creatures stand out in brilliant color, enhancing their haunting, alien quality. Also on display are penguins and sea otters. Admission. ~ Cannery Row at David Avenue; 831-648-4888, 800-756-3737, fax 831-648-4810; www.montereybayaquarium.org, e-mail equarist@monterey bayaquarium.org.

From David Avenue on the west end of Cannery Row, take Central Avenue and Ocean View Boulevard into Monterey's smaller, quieter neighboring community, **Pacific Grove**, which

Volleyball game at Lovers Point.

was originally established in 1875 as a Methodist retreat center. Alcoholic beverages were prohibited within the town limits until 1969. Today Pacific Grove remains a peaceful residential town noteworthy for its many stately Victorian-era homes and clapboard seafront cottages.

Entering Pacific Grove, you'll pass **Lovers Point Park and Beach**, with a protected swimming beach, tidepools and four-and-a-half acres of landscaped park grounds with picnic tables, restrooms, a hot dog stand and a kids' wading pool. Local historians believe the romantic-sounding name was actually shortened from Lovers of Jesus Point, as it was first called to insulate it from objections by some members of Pacific Grove's early Methodist community to public bathing. ~ Ocean View Boulevard at 17th Street, Pacific Grove.

Pacific Grove Museum of Natural History.

At the **Pacific Grove Museum of Natural History** you'll find a large exhibit hall containing mounted specimens of 291 bird species native to the Monterey Peninsula arranged in taxonomic sequence, along with a display about the life cycle of the monarch butterfly. An adjacent room features Ohlone, Salinan and Esselen Indian artifacts, about half of which were found in Monterey County, as well as a large relief map of Monterey County. The Cetacean Room has marine mammal artifacts including a humpback whale jawbone and the complete orca skeleton. Upstairs, the centerpiece of the mollusk exhibit is a preserved giant squid. There are also displays about extinct and endangered species of the area and a children's touch gallery. Outside are a native plant and wildflower garden and a life-size sculpture of a gray whale. Closed Mondays. ~ Central and Forest avenues, Pacific Grove; 831-

648-5716, fax 831-372-3256; www.pgmuseum.org, e-mail pg museum@mbay.net.

The monarch butterfly is Pacific Grove's trademark. The wooded 20-acre **George Washington Park** at the end of Junipero Avenue used to be the largest wintering ground on the California coast for the migratory butterflies. In the 1990s, however, virtually all the park's monarchs vanished. It was theorized that a storm or other natural disaster might have destroyed the butterflies during their migration, but this idea was proven wrong in 1996, when the monarchs returned to the park—but only for a single season, never to be seen again. The city has been making alterations to the park's vegetation in hopes of making it more attractive to butterflies. In the meantime, there is the small **Monarch Grove Sanctuary**, inconspicuously hidden away down a path between two residences on Ridge Road one block west of the intersection of Lighthouse Avenue and 17 Mile Drive. You'll know you're near it when you come to a pair of motels named for the monarchs. The butterflies huddle together among the sheltering leaves of eu-

Cannery Row **People**

Rereading John Steinbeck's classic novel *Cannery Row* in connection with a visit to Monterey's Cannery Row can imbue both the book and the place with a new air of authenticity. Some—and perhaps all—characters in *Cannery Row* and its sequel *Sweet Thursday* were based on real Cannery Row residents.

"Doc," the book's central character, was an accurate portrayal of pioneering marine biologist Ed Ricketts, one of Steinbeck's closest friends, who also played a central role in the author's nonfiction work *The Log of the Sea of Cortez*. A bust of Ricketts stands on the coastal trail at the corner of Wave and Drake streets, and the offshore Ed Ricketts Underwater Park stretches from the Coast Guard Pier to the Monterey Bay Aquarium.

Other *Cannery Row* characters were also thinly veiled versions of real people. Dora Flood, madame of the Bear Flag Restaurant, can only have been Flora Woods, proprietress of a brothel called the Lone Star Café. Lee Chong, who operated the grocery store of the same name, was the fictional counterpart of Won Yee, the actual proprietor of the Wing Chong Market. As for other *Cannery Row* characters such as Mack and the boys of the Palace Flophouse (a real place), they live on long after their real-life counterparts have been forgotten.

Point Pinos Lighthouse.

calyptus trees and fill the sky with flutters of orange and black on sunny days. A volunteer guide is often present to tell about the butterflies and answer questions. ~ Friends of the Monarchs, 831-375-0982.

At the tip of the peninsula, **Point Pinos Lighthouse** stands as the oldest continuously operating lighthouse on the West Coast, dating back to 1855. It originally used a lamp that burned whale oil but was electrified in 1915. The two-story house below the light tower is larger and more homey than most lighthouses, perhaps because for more than 50 years the lighthouse keepers were women. Two rooms have been restored to appear as they did in Victorian times, when Mrs. Emily Fish became known as the "socialite keeper" because of her love of entertaining guests at the lighthouse. Point Pinos Lighthouse is open to the public Thursday through Monday afternoons. ~ Lighthouse Avenue, Pacific Grove; 831-648-5716 ext. 13.

South of Point Pinos along the west side of the peninsula, **Asilomar State Beach** has over 100 acres of sugar-white-sand beach, dunes and tidepools. The same colliding northern and southern currents that make swimming dangerous also make the waters offshore unusually abundant with marine life. A trail runs the length of the beach, with boardwalks to protect the fragile dunes, which were restored after erosion had reduced

Asilomar State Beach.

them to bare rock. Across the road and also part of the park are the grounds of the historic Asilomar Conference Center (see "Not Your Typical Beach Resort" sidebar). ~ Sunset Drive, Pacific Grove; 831-372-4076, fax 831-372-3759.

The other major sightseeing highlight for visitors to the area is **17 Mile Drive**, a toll road that loops between Pacific Grove on the north and Carmel on the south. The Pacific Grove entrance is off Sunset Drive southeast of Asilomar. For details on this scenic drive, see Chapter 5.

outdoor adventures

HIKING

Urban hikers can stretch their legs along the two-mile **Path of History** or the four-mile stretch of the **Monterey Bay Recreation Trail** between Fisherman's Wharf and Lovers Point. There's also the well-hidden, surprisingly wild **Don Dahvee Memorial Trail**, which makes its way down into a wooded ravine and follows it for about a mile, curving along the edge of the Monterey Peninsula College Campus; it starts at the corner of the Don Dahvee Greenbelt, directly across the street from the Munras Avenue motel strip. The dune boardwalk at **Asilomar State Beach** in Pacific Grove also makes for a great scenic walk.

For serious forest hiking, the best place in the Monterey area is **Jacks Peak County Park**, located four miles from town. The highest point on the Monterey Peninsula, the peak was named for David Jacks, a land speculator who bought up virtually the entire peninsula in 1859 for three cents an acre in a rigged auction. (Monterey Jack cheese is also named after him.) The county park has eight miles of hiking trails that form interlocking loops along a ridgeline with minimal altitude gain. The mix-and-match hiking possibilities range from the mile-long **Skyline Nature Trail**, where interpretive signs identify the park's diverse trees, plants and wildflowers, to complex multiple-loop trips of any distance desired created by combining segments of the **Rhus Trail**, **Iris Trail**, **Sage Trail**, **Pine Trail**, **Madrone Trail** and **Earl Moser Trail**. Views of the peninsula and the ocean are the most spectacular you'll find anywhere in the Monterey Bay area. Leashed dogs are allowed on the trails, but be careful: Poison oak abounds in the area, and the most likely way to get exposed to it is to pet a dog that has gotten into it. To reach the park,

follow Route 68 for 1.6 miles east of the junction with Route 1; turn right onto Olmsted Road and go .9 mile; then turn left on Jacks Peak Road, which winds its way 1.3 miles up to the top ridge and the park entrance. ~ 831-372-8551; www.co.mon terey.ca.us/parks.

Biking along the Monterey Bay Recreation Trail.

BIKING

The **Monterey Bay Recreation Trail**, a flat, paved multiple-use trail for bikers, pedestrians and skaters, follows the north shore of the peninsula all the way from Seaside to Lovers Point, passing most of the town's major sightseeing highlights—the Municipal Wharf, Custom House Plaza, Fisherman's Wharf and Cannery Row—along the way. If the five-mile trail leaves you longing for more, continue on the bike lane alongside Ocean View Boulevard and Sunset Drive, curving around Point Pinos and continuing along Asilomar State Beach before reaching the Pacific Grove gate to 17 Mile Drive.

You can rent mountain bikes, tandems, four-wheel pedal surreys and electric bikes at **Bay Bikes**. ~ Two locations: Cannery Row, 640 Wave Street, Monterey; 831-646-9090; and Fisherman's Wharf, 99 Pacific Street; 831-655-8687; www.mon tereybaybikes.com, e-mail info@baybikes.com.

DIVING

The waters off **Asilomar State Beach** are popular for scuba diving because of the abundant sea life found in the area. It's best to go with a divemaster who knows the area well, since full exposure to the open ocean can make the water treacherously rough. **Aquarius Dive Shop** specializes in beach dives, including one- and two-tank dives and night dives. They also rent and sell gear and offer classes for beginning and advanced divers. ~ 2040 Del Monte Avenue, Monterey; 831-375-1933; www.aquariusdivers.com. Rentals and dive trips are available at **Monterey Bay Dive Center**. ~ 225 Cannery Row, Monterey; 831-656-9194, 800-607-2822; www.mbdc.to. One- and two-tank dive trips on a sailboat, as well as snorkeling expeditions, are offered by **Aquanaut**. ~ Monterey; 831-372-7245.

SURFING

The waters along the north coast of the Monterey Peninsula are too sheltered to offer the kind of spectacular surfing found elsewhere along the bay shore. However, at **Asilomar State Beach**, skilled surfers brave the hazardous currents off the main sandy beach to catch the big waves that often roll in off the open Pacific. Surfboard and wet suit rentals are available at **On the Beach Surf Shop**. 711 Cannery Row, Monterey; 831-646-9283.

SPORTFISHING

Several fishing charter boats operate from Fisherman's Wharf and Municipal Wharf #2. **Monterey Sport Fishing & Whale Watching** offers all-day trips along the rim of undersea Monterey Canyon in search of salmon, albacore and halibut. ~ 96 Old Fisherman's Wharf, Monterey; 831-372-2203, 800-200-2203; www.monte reywhalewatching.com. There's also **Randy's Fishing Trips**, with two charter boats. Advance reservations recommended.

~ 66 Old Fisherman's Wharf, Monterey; 831-372-7440. **Sam's Fishing Fleet** also offers day charters. ~ 84 Old Fisherman's Wharf, Monterey; 831-372-0577. **Top Gun Sportfishing** takes small groups for half-day fishing trips on a 65-foot boat. ~ 90 Old Fisherman's Wharf, Monterey; 831-372-8500; www.top gunsportfishing.com.

Anglers fish for rockfish and surf perch from Monterey's Municipal Wharf #2 and from the small pier at Lovers Point in Pacific Grove; no license required. Bait and tackle are available at **The Compass Boat & Fishing Supplies**. ~ Fisherman's Wharf, Monterey; 831-647-9222.

WHALE WATCHING

All the charter boat operators listed above under "Sportfishing" also offer whale-watching tours during the early-December-to-early-April gray whale migration. **Chris' Whale Watching Tours**, the oldest and largest operation on Monterey Bay, operates four boats year-round, searching for gray whales in winter and humpback and blue whales the rest of the year. ~ 48 Fisherman's Wharf, Monterey; 831-375-5951; www.chrisswhalewatching.com. Tours led by marine biologists are available at **Monterey Bay Whale Watch**.

Kayaking on Monterey Bay.

~ Fisherman's Wharf, Monterey; 831-375-4658; www.mon tereybaywhalewatch.com. **Scenic Bay Sailing School & Yacht Charters** takes whale-watching groups out on its sailboat. ~ Monterey Municipal Marina; 831-372-6603.

KAYAKING

The protected, usually calm waters around Monterey Municipal Harbor and Cannery Row present good opportunities for kayakers who don't mind the urban setting. A more natural, equally sheltered coastline extends in both directions from Lovers Point in Pacific Grove. Guided natural-history tours of Monterey Bay, as well as rentals and classes, are available at **Monterey Bay Kayaks**. ~ 693 Del Monte Avenue, Monterey; 831-373-5357, 800-649-5357; www.monterey baykayaks.com. Another large kayak rental operation, which offers two- to three-hour tours along Cannery Row with a marine biologist, is **Adventures by the Sea**. ~ 299 Cannery Row, Monterey; 831-372-1807; www.adventures bythesea.com. Cannery Row kayak rentals are also available at **A B Seas Kayaks of Monterey**. ~ 32 Cannery Row, Monterey; 831-647-0147. And there are sea kayaks for rent on the beach at Lovers Point on a first-come, first-served basis. ~ Ocean View Boulevard at 17th Street, Pacific Grove.

WHAT HAPPENED TO ALL THE SARDINES?

Talk about killing the goose that laid golden eggs! Once Monterey was known as the sardine capital of the world. Sardines were so plentiful in Monterey Bay that they could be scooped up by the handful or caught in a basket just a few feet from shore. The supply of the tiny fish was thought to be inexhaustible. But in response to the food shortages of World War II, the government lifted its quotas on sardine fishing, and within three years all the sardines in the Monterey Bay area were wiped out. Today, only one Monterey cannery still processes sardines—which are brought in from other California fishing ports.

GOLF

Opened in 1897, Monterey's **Del Mar Golf Course** has the distinction of being the oldest course in continuous operation west of the Mississippi River. With its me-

MEXICAN MONTEREY

In 1822 Mexico won its independence from Spain, and the property of wealthy loyalists was seized and given to leaders who had supported the Mexican cause. Mexico also opened its borders to U.S. settlers— which turned out to be a mistake. In May 1846, American settlers revolted against the Mexicans and renamed California the Bear Flag Republic. It remained an independent nation for only two months before the peace treaty ending the Mexican War awarded California to the United States, and U.S. Navy vessels arrived to take control of the capital.

andering, hilly layout, tree-lined fairways and small, well-protected greens, it is still considered to be a challenging course. The 6339-yard par-72 course hosts the California State Amateur Tour. Club and cart rentals are available. ~ 1300 Sylvan Road, Monterey; 831-373-2700.

In the Monterey suburb of Seaside, the **Bayonet and Black Horse Golf Courses** formerly operated as an exclusive club and have been cited as favorites by golf superstars such as Arnold Palmer, Jack Nicklaus and Tiger Woods. The 7009-yard par-69 Black Horse course offers thrilling ocean views from every hole, rivaling even Pebble Beach for scenery, and presents a kaleidoscope of challenges that will give you a chance to use every club in your bag. Bayonet has no water hazards and few traps or bunkers, yet the 7117-yard par-72 course with its narrow pine-flanked fairways is ranked one of the most difficult in the area. You'll find out why as you attempt the famous fairway known as "Combat Corner." Cart rentals are available. ~ 1 McClure Way, Seaside; 831-899-7271; www.bbhgolf.com.

Seven miles east of Monterey, the **Laguna Seca Golf Club** was designed by Robert Trent Jones. An exceptionally tricky 6157-yard par-71 course, its sudden elevation changes, strategically placed sand traps and water hazards, and dogleg greens flanked by dense stands of oak make this a course no golfer should miss. The clubhouse has a full dining room. Clubs and carts are available for rent. Green fees are surprisingly reasonable compared to other Monterey Peninsula courses. ~ 10520 York Road, Monterey; 831-373-3701, 888-524-8629; www.golf-monterey.com.

Opened in 1932, the **Pacific Grove Municipal Golf Links** were created in the style of traditional Scottish links, following a relatively straight course paralleling the ocean from Point Pinos. The front nine holes of the 5732-yard par-70 course go through the forest, while the back nine are bordered by sand dunes. Club rentals are available. ~ 77 Asilomar Boulevard; 831-648-3175, fax 831-648-3179.

CAMPING

The only campground, public or private, in the immediate Monterey area is at **Veterans Memorial Park**, set in 50 acres of forest and landscaped park lawn on the Monterey skyline. The view of Monterey and the bay is stupendous. There are 40 tent/RV sites with restrooms and pay showers but no hookups. Sites cost $15 per night, first-come, first-served. Open year-round. ~ Skyline Drive at Jefferson Street; 831-646-3865.

Situated about seven miles east of Monterey, **Laguna Seca Recreation Area** has 175 tent/RV sites in the grassy, oak-studded hills adjacent to the famous Laguna Seca Speedway auto and motorcycle racetrack. Sites have picnic tables and fire grills. Most have level concrete RV pads, and many have water and electric hookups. Campground facilities include restrooms, pay showers and a dump station. Also in the park are a small lake and a shooting range. Sites cost $18 to $22 per night. Open year-round. ~ Route 68; 831-758-3604, fax 831-755-6818; reservations 831-755-4899, 888-588-2267; www.co.monterey. ca.us/parks.

Monterey.

lodging

All accommodations in Monterey tend to be booked solid on weekends, so it's a good idea to make reservations well in advance. During the week you can usually reserve a room almost anywhere on short notice, and you can usually find a vacancy at one of the motels along Munras Avenue without a reservation. To find out what's available with a single phone call, contact **Resort II Me**, a free reservation service that represents most lodgings on the peninsula. ~ 831-642-6622, 800-757-5646, fax 831-642-6641; www.resort2me.com, e-mail info@resort2me.com.

Most reasonably priced lodgings in Monterey are found in a solid strip of motels along the west side of Munras Avenue. The **Adobe Inn** is a typical example, except that it's the only motel along the row that accepts pets. The two-story complex (which is not really made of adobe) has 26 clean, contemporary guest rooms with the standard amenities, as well as a swimming pool and whirlpool. Across the street is an attractive park with a pretty, inconspicuous foot trail through a tree-shrouded ravine. ~ 936 Munras Avenue, Monterey; 831-372-5409, fax 831-375-7236. BUDGET TO MODERATE.

A showpiece B&B on a quiet side street just a short walk from the Path of History and downtown Monterey, the **Old Monterey Inn** is a 1929 Tudor-style mansion on a wooded hillside. The inn has seven one-bedroom units and three luxury suites, some with whirlpool tubs. All rooms have wicker furniture, feather beds and private baths, and some have fireplaces. Amenities include CD players and VCRs, and the inn has an extensive video library. The room rate includes a lavish gourmet breakfast—they'll even serve it to you in bed. ~ 500 Martin Street, Monterey; 831-375-8284, 800-350-2344, fax 831-375-6730; www.oldmontereyinn.com, e-mail omi@oldmontereyinn.com. ULTRA-DELUXE.

The **Merritt House**, a 25-room bed and breakfast, is a point of interest along the Path of History. The two-story adobe main house was originally built by a Spanish don in 1774. It later became the home of Judge Josiah Merritt, a

OPPOSITE: Old Monterey Inn.

major political figure during the period just after California became part of the United States, and was "modernized" with columned wood facade. In converting the house to an inn, the new owners added a modern annex. The rooms in both the old house and the annex have fireplaces, balconies, lofty ceilings and hardwood period furnishings. Gardens surrounding the house feature rose bushes and fig, olive, pepper and magnolia trees. ~ 386 Pacific Street, Monterey; 831-646-9686, 800-541-5599, fax 831-646-5392; www.merritthouseinn.com, e-mail

info@merritthouseinn.com. DE-LUXE TO ULTRA-DELUXE.

Steinbeck enthusiasts will find luxury lodgings centrally located on Cannery Row at the four-story, 42-unit **Spindrift Inn**. It sure ain't the Palace Flophouse. The stylish lobby features hand-tiled floors, oriental carpets, antiques and original sculp-

Spindrift Inn.

tures; a rooftop solarium overlooks the water. Rooms have hardwood floors, down featherbeds, fireplaces and marble-and-brass baths; some have bay windows overlooking the bay. Room rates include a continental breakfast served in your room on a silver platter, as well as afternoon wine and cheese. ~ 652 Cannery Row, Monterey; 831-646-8900, 800-232-4141, fax 831-646-5342; www.spindriftinn.com, e-mail reservations@innsofmonterey.com. ULTRA-DELUXE.

Located in a neighborhood of stately Victorian houses, the **Green Gables Inn** in Pacific Grove is one of the Monterey Peninsula's most elegant B&Bs. The 1888 Queen Anne–style main house, with step gables, gingerbread trim and stained glass, stands on a hillside overlooking the bay. Four of the five upstairs guest rooms share two baths but have the best views of the water. There are also a spacious ground-floor suite and five more rooms in a modern annex. All rooms are decorated with antiques and have king- or queen-size beds; some have whirlpool baths or fireplaces. Rates include afternoon wine and cheese and a full breakfast. ~ 104 5th Street, Pacific Grove; 831-375-2095, 800-722-1774, fax 831-375-5437; www.foursisters. com, e-mail info@foursisters.com. DELUXE TO ULTRA-DELUXE.

Fabulous ocean views are the key feature of the **Martine Inn**, a Mediterranean-style stucco villa on the waterfront. Many of the 25 individually decorated rooms have fireplaces and views of the water. Among them is the unique Edith Head Room, furnished with 1920s-vintage items from the legendary Hollywood costume designer's estate. Rates include a full breakfast and afternoon hors d'oeuvres. The minimum stay is two nights. ~ 255 Ocean View Boulevard, Pacific Grove; 831-373-3388, 800-852-5588, fax 831-373-3896; www.martineinn. com, e-mail info@martineinn.com. ULTRA-DELUXE.

Not Your Typical Beach Resort

Certainly the most unusual lodging option in the Monterey area, **Asilomar Conference Center** is set among the sand dunes and pine forests of Pacific Grove's Asilomar State Park, directly across the road from the peninsula's best beach. Guests are likely to see deer wandering the grounds. Originally built in 1913 as a

YWCA retreat, Asilomar has grown to 30 buildings containing a total of 313 guest rooms in a campuslike setting. Some of the redwood-and-stone structures are National Historic Landmarks designed by famed architects Julia Morgan (who also created Hearst Castle) and John Carl Warnecke (best known for the John F. Kennedy Memorial). Accommodations come in a variety of styles
and configurations. Those in the older buildings feature hardwood floors and brass beds, while newer ones have carpeted floors. All lodgings have private baths, and many buildings have common living rooms with fireplaces and overstuffed chairs. While Asilomar is operated primarily for groups (which reserve their space as much as five years in advance), it rents rooms to individual travelers as space permits. None of the guest rooms have telephones or televisions. ~ 800 Asilomar Boulevard, Pacific Grove; 831-372-8016, fax 831-372-7227; www.asilomarcenter.com, e-mail asilomarsales@dncinc.com. MODERATE TO DELUXE.

Gosby House Inn.

The **Gosby House Inn**, a yellow Victorian mansion that has been welcoming guests for more than 100 years, has 22 cozy, individually decorated rooms, each with unique antique touches—a canopy bed here, a Tiffany lamp there, or perhaps a clawfoot tub. Some have jacuzzis, fireplaces, window seats or private patio entrances. The full breakfast includes home-baked bread. Tea, wine and sherry are served in the afternoon. ~ 643 Lighthouse Avenue, Pacific Grove; 831-375-1287, 800-527-8828, fax 831-655-9621; www.foursisters.com, e-mail info@foursisters.com. MODERATE TO DELUXE.

Several standard motels cluster near the Monarch Grove Sanctuary. The two-story **Butterfly Grove Inn** has 28 units, some with whirlpools and fireplaces, all with microwaves. There's a heated outdoor pool and a videotape rental library. A two-night minimum stay is required on weekends. ~ 1073 Lighthouse Avenue, Pacific Grove; 831-373-4921, 800-337-9244, fax 831-373-7596; www.butterflygroveinn.com. MODERATE.

dining

You'll get a full serving of Old Monterey ambience along with food that the *San Francisco Chronicle* has called the best in Monterey at **Stokes Restaurant & Bar**. The Mexican-era adobe building dating back to 1833 is decorated with European antiques and works by local artists. The menu features fare that ranges from tapas such as fava bean crostini and sardine *escabeche* to full meals of steaks, chops or crispy duck breast, as well as wood-fired heirloom-tomato pizzas. The focus is on locally grown organic produce, seafood and wild mushrooms. No lunch on Sundays. ~ 500

Hartnell Street, Monterey; 831-373-1110, fax 831-373-1202; www.stokesrestaurant.com, e-mail stokes@mbay.net. MODERATE TO DELUXE.

A standout among Monterey's Asian eateries, **Won Ju Korean Restaurant** offers authentic, meticulously prepared dishes such as *bi bim bap* and *kalbi,* with *kim chee* (pickled cabbage) or sesame spinach on the side. Dinners come with potato pancakes or rice. ~ 570 Lighthouse Avenue, Monterey; 831-656-0672. MODERATE TO DELUXE.

Fun Italian ambience sets **Gianni's Pizza** apart from run-of-the-mill pizza joints. Brick false archways on the back wall frame murals of Venetian canals. A gelato cart rests among the assorted wine bottles, classic red-and-white checkered tablecloths and Italian bric-a-brac make up the decor. On weekends, strolling musicians serenade diners with upbeat accordion tunes. Pizzas ranging from 8 to 18 inches in diameter can be ordered with one or several toppings from a list of more than two dozen options, including all the standards as well as a few surprises (linguica, spinach, chicken, jalapeños and pesto sauce). No lunch on Mondays through Thursdays. ~ 725 Lighthouse Avenue, Monterey; 831-649-1500. BUDGET TO MODERATE.

Stokes Restaurant & Bar.

A standout among the numerous tourist-oriented restaurants on Fisherman's Wharf, the casual **Abalonetti** specializes

in squid, the inky little arrowhead-shaped cousins of octopi that abound in Monterey Bay and can be found in many local restaurants under the euphemistically European name "calamari." Here you can try calamari in a wide range of recipes—grilled as filets, deep-fried, sautéed with wine and

A calamari offering from Abalonetti.

garlic or baked with eggplant. Fish specials round out the menu. ~ 57 Fisherman's Wharf, Monterey; 831-373-1851, fax 831-373-2058. MODERATE TO ULTRA-DELUXE.

A mesquite-fired brick pizza oven is among the distinctive features of **Café Fina**, a small, casual, Italian-flavored restaurant on Fisherman's Wharf with intimate upstairs and downstairs dining areas. In addition to gourmet pizzas with toppings that include smoked salmon and baby shrimp, there's a tempting selection of seafood dishes including grilled sanddabs, calamari steak and petrale sole almondine. ~ 47 Fisherman's Wharf, Monterey; 831-372-5200; www.cafefina.com, e-mail info@cafe fina.com. DELUXE.

A small restaurant conceived with gourmet dining in mind, **Fresh Cream** is set on Heritage Harbor, with floor-to-ceiling windows that look out toward Fisherman's Wharf. French prints and leaded glass decorate the muted gray and pastel green walls to create an air of understated elegance. The bill of fare changes daily and usually includes many of the restaurant's hallmark dishes such as grilled white veal loin with sherry creamed mushrooms, pan-seared ahi in pineapple rum sauce, duckling in black currant sauce and rack of lamb. Dinner only. ~ Pacific and Scott streets, Monterey; 831-375-9798; www.fresh cream.com, e-mail dining@freshcream.com. ULTRA-DELUXE.

Coffee connoisseurs should make a beeline for **Plume's Coffee**, a one-of-a-kind café where you can select and mix your own blend of beans, then have it individually ground and brewed just for you. To accompany your custom-made cuppa java, choose from an array of pastries, fruit tarts, eclairs, cheesecakes and other delights from one of Monterey's best bakeries. ~ 400 Alvarado Street, Monterey; 831-373-4526. BUDGET.

Cannery Row has emerged as Monterey's premier dining district. For instance, **Clawdaddy's Restaurant**, located upstairs overlooking Cannery Row's Steinbeck Plaza, strives for a Bourbon Street ambience with brick floors, Mardi Gras beads and indoor street lights. The fare is somewhat Cajun, often combining routine steak and pasta fare with spicy bayou side dishes. Standouts include blackened swordfish steak with Creole sauce and shrimp étouffée. Try the Cajun-style marinated and grilled Castroville artichoke appetizer. For lunch there are fish po'boys and other sandwiches. ~ 660 Cannery Row, Monterey; 831-648-8500; www.clawdaddys.com. MODERATE TO DELUXE.

A longtime Cannery Row favorite in the renovated shell of an old canning factory, the **Fish Hopper** has an oyster bar, plenty of potted plants and an outdoor deck over the bay. Menu highlights include steak-and-lobster specials and a unique sea-

••

School for Fine Dining

While many restaurants on Cannery Row offer seafood-and-pasta menus and prices that are almost identical, this is certainly not the case at **Mary's International Restaurant**, part of the highly regarded Culinary Center of Monterey cooking school. Set in the Old Custom House (not the same as the Custom House near Fisherman's Wharf on the Path of History) with its original weatherbeaten, fire-scarred exposed wood beams, Mary's offers dining on an outside terrace above the water or indoors by the fireplace in the white-walled, contemporary café-style dining area. All dishes are prepared by faculty members of the cooking school, and most represent culinary styles taught at the school, including such international fusion masterpieces as pan-seared scallops in four-pepper cream sauce and New York strip steak with *chimichurri*. The restaurant also serves Saturday and Sunday brunch buffets and Friday-night all-you-can-eat seafood buffets. Picnic lunches and gourmet take-home dinners are also available. ~ 625 Cannery Row #200, Monterey; 831-333-2133; www.culinarycenterofmonterey.com, e-mail info@culinarycenterofmonterey.com. MODERATE TO DELUXE.

••

scallop-and-crab-meat casserole. ~ 700 Cannery Row, Monterey; 831-372-8543; www.fishhopper.com. MODERATE.

The most exclusive restaurant in the Cannery Row area, one block inland on Wave Street, the **Sardine Factory** bucks the ultra-casual trend of most Monterey restaurants with a semi-formal dress code and four individually and lavishly decorated dining rooms, including one with a purple-and-gold color scheme that some patrons may find regal but others may see as the gaudiest decor this side of Vegas. The service is impeccable, and the bill of fare features imaginative seafood dishes such as Monterey Bay sea bass on a bed of wild chanterelle mushrooms and a cioppino (Italian-style seafood stew) of crabs, prawns, mussels, clams, scallops, fish and sun-dried calamari in tomato broth. Reservations are essential. ~ 701 Wave Street, Monterey; 831-373-2818; www.sardinefactory.com, e-mail info@sardinefactory.com. DELUXE TO ULTRA-DELUXE.

The white walls and tablecloths of **The Tinnery** in Pacific Grove present little distraction from the restaurant's spectacular views of the Pacific and Lovers Point Park. American-style seafood, including some of the best clam chowder on the

peninsula, is the main focus of the menu, which also includes pasta dishes such as seafood linguini in alfredo sauce and non-seafood selections such as chicken California—a boneless breast of chicken stuffed with Monterey Jack cheese and avocado and smothered in champagne cream sauce. Breakfast, lunch and dinner are served. ~ 631 Ocean View Boulevard, Pacific Grove; 831-646-1040, fax 831-646-5913. MODERATE TO DELUXE.

Across the street, the more upscale **Old Bath House Restaurant** boasts ornate decor showcasing etched glass

Old Bath House Restaurant.

and a Victorian-style bar. The fare features steak, lobster, seafood, lamb and duckling prepared in culinary stylings that walk the line between Continental and California cuisine. Dinner only. ~ 620 Ocean View Boulevard, Pacific Grove; 831-375-5195, fax 831-375-5379; www. oldbathhouse.com, e-mail lvrspt@ aol.com. DELUXE TO ULTRA-DELUXE.

Surveying the multitude of restaurants geared toward out-of-town visitors in the Monterey and Pacific Grove area, one may wonder where local folks eat. The answer is the **Red House Café**, a cozy place that serves breakfast, lunch

Red House Café.

and dinner in a friendly, casual setting. Not that this is your typical bacon-and-eggs kind of place; breakfast options include Belgian waffles, frittatas and croissant sandwiches. Lunch and dinner offerings range from roast chicken sandwiches to warm eggplant with fontina cheese. A specialty of the house is freshly squeezed lemonade—with free refills. No dinner on Sundays. Closed Mondays. ~ 662 Lighthouse Avenue, Pacific Grove; 831-643-1060; www.redhousecafe.com, e-mail info@redhouse cafe.com. BUDGET TO MODERATE.

Simplicity and charm go arm-in-arm with imaginative cooking at **Passionfish**, a small gourmet place with a big wine list and a menu that changes daily. Try a house special of the day or one of the restaurant's tried-and-true entrées such as duck confit with Tasmanian honey sauce or mahimahi with Vietnamese dipping sauce, or savor the Passionfish stew—a generous helping of mixed seafood in butternut squash broth. Dinner only. ~ 701 Lighthouse Avenue, Pacific Grove; 831-655-3311; www.passionfish.net, e-mail massion@passionfish. net. MODERATE TO DELUXE.

●●●

Spanish Monterey

Monterey, like many California cities, got its start as a Catholic mission and Spanish military presidio in 1770. Although the church was later moved to the far side of the peninsula to put some distance between its converts and the Presidio's soldiers, the king of Spain declared Monterey the capital of Alta (upper) California in 1775. It had no civilian population at the time, so conquistador Don Juan Bautista de Anza set out from Mexico City, leading a group of 240 settlers with livestock, farming implements and household goods. Monterey was the capital for the next 70 years, outlasting the Spanish colonial presence in the New World.

●●●

A step beyond typical Mexican restaurants, **Peppers Mexicali Café** celebrates chile peppers as an edible art form and one of the five major food groups. Chile posters and pepper prints by local artists decorate the walls, and you'll probably have plenty of time to appreciate them, since the wait for a table—especially at lunch hour—can be nearly eternal. Worth waiting for, the fare highlights Latin American seafood stylings such as *huachinango* Veracruz, grilled seafood tacos and grilled prawns with fresh lime and cilantro dressing. No lunch on Sundays. Closed Tuesdays. ~ 170 Forest Avenue, Pacific Grove; 831-373-6892, fax 831-373-5467. BUDGET TO MODERATE.

nightlife
●●●●●●●●●●●●●●●●

Kalisa's La Ida Café hosts Belly Dancing Extravaganzas on Friday evenings from 8 p.m. to midnight and serves wine, beer and espresso. You pay a cover charge and, in exchange, receive coupons for free food. Kalisa Moore, the "Queen of Cannery Row" who has operated La Ida's since 1958, sometimes makes personal appearances in the evenings to reminisce about the good old days with audiences of Steinbeck buffs. ~ 851 Cannery Row, Monterey; 831-644-9316.

The liveliest nightspot in Monterey, **Club Octane** is a multilevel club with three dancefloors featuring deejay dance music and sometimes live performances. There are also occasional strip shows; call for the current show schedule. Oh, yes, and wear "fashionable club attire" or you may not make it past the doorman. Cover. ~ 321-D Alvarado Street, Monterey; 831-646-9244.

Nicknamed "the Cheers of Monterey," **Viva Monterey** combines a packed pool hall with a dancefloor presenting live bands. Cover. ~ 414 Alvarado Street, Monterey; 831-646-1415.

Known among locals as the last gay bar in Monterey, the **Lighthouse Bar & Grill** actually caters to an interesting mix of gay and straight patrons with cocktails and pub food. There are pool tables, pinball machines, a romantic patio and a big-screen TV that blares Monday Night Football in season. ~ 281 Lighthouse Avenue, Monterey; 831-373-4488.

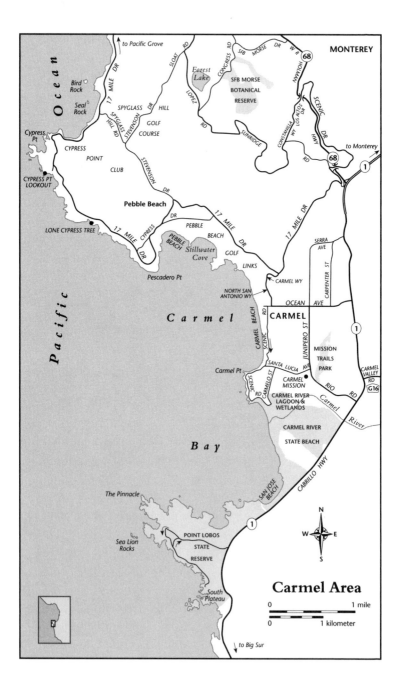

Carmel Area

```
0                                    1 mile

0                                    1 kilometer
```

5

Carmel

One-tenth the size of Monterey, Carmel-by-the-Sea is one of California's most unusual communities. Built on the site of a former Spanish colonial mission, the village was conceived around the beginning of the century by San Jose real estate broker Frank Devendorf, who had built a small resort hotel near the beach and envisioned it surrounded by a family village inhabited by California's leading artists, writers, scientists and thinkers. He offered to sell lots in his future village to select individuals at near-giveaway prices, conveying the first lot to a black woman because he hoped ethnic and cultural diversity would be a hallmark of the new community.

Carmel-by-the-Sea got off to a slow start—after all, it was in a very remote area without public utilities of any kind, and at first the residents lived in tents—but after the earthquake of 1906 many well-known artists and writers fled San Francisco and found their way to this idyllic seaside setting, and Devendorf's dream became a full-blown reality almost overnight. Among the early residents were poet Robinson Jeffers, novelists Sinclair Lewis, Mary Austin and Upton Sinclair, and photographers Ansel Adams and Edward Weston. Jack London and Ambrose Bierce also spent time there.

In addition to its natural virtues, newcomers to Carmel discovered that it enjoyed one of the nicest climates on the central California coast,

Point Joe.

averaging ten degrees warmer than Monterey Bay or San Francisco—and sunnier, averaging 283 days of sunshine a year.

Devendorf was a visionary, but he was nobody's fool. From the start, he planned for Carmel-by-the-Sea to have a prosperous tourist economy that would not only keep his resort hotel filled but also support a commercial district of art galleries and performing-arts venues. This, too, came to pass—and to surpass Devendorf's wildest imaginings. Today Carmel-by-the-Sea boasts one of California's most elite shopping areas. Not only that, the state's wealthiest individuals also come to shop for real estate. As a result, property values in the Carmel area have skyrocketed to a level where few of the artists exhibited in the village's galleries can afford to live there.

In the mid-20th century, the official name Carmel-by-the-Sea was abbreviated to simply Carmel. Recently, however, as the wealthy populace of Carmel has spread out into nearby areas (Carmel Valley, an idyllic vision of pastoral California where horse ranches and tennis courts take the place of the giant farm machinery, vast vegetable fields, migrant workers or pesticides

Carmel Mission.

that characterize other agricultural areas of the state, and Carmel Highlands, where developers raced to fill the rocky bluffs south of Point Lobos with multimillion-dollar glass-front mansions just ahead of the California Coastal Act of 1976, which severely restricted coastal development) the original village has returned to the name Carmel-by-the-Sea to distinguish itself from its suburbs.

The natural beauty of the Carmel area offers a wealth of opportunities for hiking and cycling.

View from 17 Mile Drive.

The ultra-exclusive adjoining area of Pebble Beach, the only community in America that you have to pay an admission fee to drive through, seems to consist mainly of golf courses, including some of the most famous in the country—a true fantasyland for duffers who, if they can't actually reserve a hard-to-get tee time or afford the astronomical green fees, can at least drive by Pebble Beach and Spyglass Hill and daydream before heading off to one of the less rarified courses in the Monterey Bay area.

The most direct way to reach Carmel-by-the-Sea is to exit Route 1 on Ocean Avenue, the main commercial boulevard and a key landmark. Directions to anyplace in the one-mile-square village, which has no street addresses, usually start with "North (or south) of Ocean."

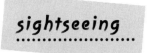

sightseeing

The approach from Route 1 is one of two routes into Carmel-by-the-Sea. The other, which is ideal for visitors coming from Pacific Grove on a grand tour of the Monterey Peninsula, is **17 Mile Drive**. This scenic route has three main entrances: the Pacific Grove Gate off Sunset Drive just east of the Asilomar Conference Center, the Highway One Gate exit north of Ocean Avenue and the Carmel Gate on North San Antonio near the west end of Ocean Avenue.

17 Mile Drive leads through **Pebble Beach**, a community so exclusive that visitors have to pay just to drive through it. Dream houses stand secluded amid a wilderness forest of Gowen and Monterey cypress protected by building restrictions imposed by Pebble Beach's founder, Samuel Finley Breeze Morse (a distant relative of the Samuel F. B. Morse who invented the telegraph). "Profits," Morse declared, "are incidental to the orderly projection of subdivisions that will not mar the rare beauty of this place. Pebble Beach is one spot on 1100 miles of gorgeous coastline which will remain completely unspoiled." Morse's environmental concern, however, did not prevent him from razing expanses of forest to build the first of five golf courses that now occupy nearly half the land area of Pebble Beach.

When driving from Pacific Grove, the first point of interest you'll come to is **Spanish Bay**, where explorer Juan Gaspar de Portolá landed in 1769, claiming central California for the

Cypress Point.

• •

Town without Numbers

One of Carmel-by-the-Sea's many endearing eccentricities is the absence of street addresses. It was the opinion of founder Frank Devendorf that numbers might distract the creative energies of the artists, writers, inventors and thinkers he was trying to attract to his new colony. (Most avenues were numbered, however, to keep visitors from becoming completely lost.) A conflict arose when the California legislature passed a law requiring every residence and business in the state to have a numbered address. The lawmakers assented to an unwritten exception for Carmel-by-the-Sea after the village publically threatened to secede from California and declare itself an independent country. Though the threat was as impractical as most everything else about Carmel, the publicity surrounding it did wonders for the village's tourist trade.

• •

Spanish Empire and setting the stage for the establishment of Carmel Mission the following year. Today a golf course and luxury inn occupy the site. **Moss Beach**, which fronts on Spanish Bay, is a favorite picnic area, as is nearby **Point Joe**, where Chinese settlers established a fishing village in the 1890s, building their houses of wood salvaged from the numerous ships that wrecked off the point after mistaking it for the entrance to Monterey Bay.

Bird Rock and **Seal Rock**, as their names suggest, are refuges for harbor seals and California sea lions as well as cormorants, pelicans and other birds. Across the road, the **Bird Rock Hunt Course** has traditionally been used for foxhunts and steeplechase competitions and also served as a U.S. Cavalry training base during the 1920s.

Continuing southward, 17 Mile Drive skirts the edge of **Spyglass Hill Golf Course**, the famed links designed by Robert Trent Jones and named for a setting in Robert Louis Stevenson's classic novel *Treasure Island.* The road then passes another golf course, the **Cypress Point Club**, on its way to two scenic vistas: **Fanshell Overlook**, with its view to the north of a pristine white-sand beach where harbor seals come to birth their pups in spring, and **Cypress Point Lookout**, a view so classically photogenic that you may feel as if you've been here before simply because its image has appeared in so many magazines and coffee-table books.

Lone Cypress.

Farther down the road, past the 13-acre **Crocker Grove** nature reserve, is an even more familiar vista—the **Lone Cypress**. This twisted old tree on its rocky promontory has actually been registered as a trademark of the Pebble Beach Company, and anyone who publishes a photo of it, even on the internet, is likely to hear from some high-priced attorneys.

Farther along the coastline are the **Ghost Tree**, a salt-bleached, wind-warped old cypress whose image is not protected by law, and **Pescadero Point**, the southernmost extent of the Monterey Peninsula. From there, you'll proceed past the **Pebble Beach Golf Links** and the **Lodge at Pebble Beach** and soon arrive at 17 Mile Drive's Carmel Gate.

17 Mile Drive continues beyond the Carmel Gate to end at the Highway 1 Gate, but the tour route through Pebble Beach loops back to Spanish Bay by way of a marked route following Sunridge Road, Scenic Drive, Los Altos Drive, Sunridge Road (again), Lopez Road and Sloat Road. Following this inland route, you'll climb up **Shepherd's Knoll** for a magnificent view of the Monterey Peninsula and coastline, then up **Huckleberry Hill**, a densely forested ridge that separates Carmel from Pacific Grove. Passing **Poppy Hills Golf Course**, you'll

wend your way past little **Forest Lake** and among wooded estates back to the Pacific Grove Gate.

Whichever route you take to get to Carmel-by-the-Sea, as you drive along **Ocean Avenue** with its trendy galleries and cute cafés, you may suspect that the main reason visitors come here is to spend money—lots of it—but you'd be only partly right. To discover the "real" Carmel, park your car and walk the narrow, sidewalkless back streets where many of the quaint old-time cottages and lush gardens that originally created the village's distinctive character can still be found. There are pay parking lots at Sunset Center (Mission Street and 8th Avenue) and Carmel Plaza (Mission Street between Ocean and 7th avenues), as well as free municipal parking at Vista Lobos Park

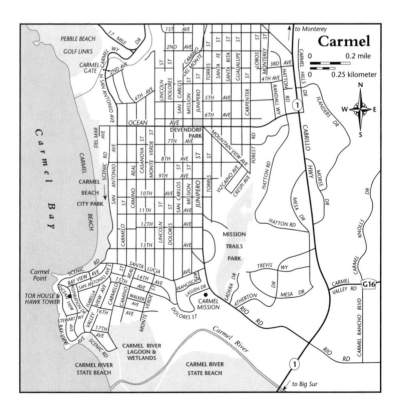

(Torres Street and 3rd Avenue). There are no parking meters on the streets, but be aware that the 90-minute on-street parking limit is strictly enforced.

The residential areas of the village reveal the collective imagination of the artists' colony that was Carmel in the early 20th century. Strolling the side streets will take you past block after block of fairytale Tudor Revival cottages, handbuilt adobe structures, miniature castles, whimsical gingerbread Victorians, at least one Frank Lloyd Wright creation and such oddities as a house constructed from shipwreck salvage and another made entirely of doors. There are bright flower gardens and secret courtyards everywhere. Most of the homes are cozy because the lots given away to the colony's first residents were small, but here and there an old cottage has been added onto on such a grand scale that it has grown into a majestic residence filling every square inch of the property—testament to the ongoing struggle between locals who seek to preserve the village's historic character and a steady influx of wealthy newcomers who try to blend ostentation into their notion of Carmel charm. It's a kaleidoscope of quaintness, a beachfront Never-Never Land, a hobbit shire for the very rich.

Tor House.

At the foot of Ocean Avenue is **Carmel Beach**, a white-sand seashore paradise that may well be the most beautiful strand on the central California coast. Sheltered by cypress trees, the beach is out of sight of any commercialism even though it's just steps away from the heart of town. Running south from Ocean Avenue parallel to the beach, the meandering, sometimes hair-raising Scenic Road leads past **Tor House and Hawk Tower**, two medieval-looking stone edifices. They were built in the 1920s by poet Robinson Jeffers, a central figure in Carmel's literary community at the time. Built entirely of quarried granite, Tor house was patterned after an English-style stone barn, and Hawk Tower

Opposite: Carmel Beach.

with its six-foot-thick walls was modeled on an Irish tower. One-hour tours of the house and tower are available by reservation on Fridays and Saturdays. No children under 12 allowed. Admission. ~ 26304 Ocean View Avenue; 831-624-1813, fax 831-624-3696; www.torhouse.org, e-mail thf@torhouse.org.

Continuing past Tor House and Hawk Tower, Scenic Road brings you to **Carmel River Lagoon and Wetlands** and, on the other side of the river, **Carmel River State Beach**. The Carmel River is impounded in Carmel Valley to form San Clemente and Los Padre reservoirs, and as a result there is normally not enough water to flow over the sandbar at its mouth and into the bay. On rare occasions when heavy rains bring a threat of flooding, the state dredges a temporary channel through the sand to let excess water escape to the sea. The rest of the time, the river ends in a freshwater lagoon that provides an ideal habitat for willets, sandpipers, pelicans, hawks, kingfishers, herons and migrating snow geese. The sandy beach has restrooms. ~ End of Carmelo Road; 831-624-4909, fax 831-624-9265.

Carmel River State Beach.

Carmel Valley Wine Tasting

The exceptional microclimate of the Carmel Valley, with its relatively warm temperatures and sunshine combined with moist sea breezes, has given rise to a growing number of prestigious wineries, and a scenic drive up Carmel Valley Road makes for one of the most enjoyable wine-tasting excursions in the state. The first one you'll come to is **Château Julien Wine Estate**, where tours are available twice daily by reservation only. ~ 8940 Carmel Valley Road; 831-624-2600, fax 831-624-6138; www.chateaujulien.com. Farther along, in the vicinity of Carmel Valley Village, are a cluster of vineyards and winery tasting rooms, including the **Bernardus Winery**, with a tasting room open daily. ~ 5 West Carmel Valley Road; 831-659-1900, 800-223-2533, fax 831-659-1676; www.bernardus.com. The **Heller Estate** grows organic grapes for cabernet sauvignon, chardonnay, merlot, pinot noir, chenin blanc and riesling. ~ 69 West Carmel Valley Road; 831-659-6220, 800-625-8466, fax 831-659-6226; www.heller estate.com. **Joullian Vineyards** produces similar offerings, along with Carmel Valley's first and only zinfandel; tasting fee, $3. ~ 2 Village Drive, Carmel Valley; 831-659-8100, 877-659-2800, fax 831-659-2802; www.joullian.com. The **Talbott Tasting Room** presents estate-grown wines for sample and sale. ~ 53 West

Château Julien Wine Estate.

Carmel Valley Road; 831-659-3500, fax 831-659-3515; www.talbottvineyards.com. Last but not least, **Galante Vineyards** is known for producing some of the finest premium cabernet sauvignon in California. They host special events, and tours are available by reservation. The vineyards are located up a narrow road with tight turns; allow plenty of time to get there. ~ 18181 Cachagua Road, Carmel Valley; 800-425-2683, fax 831-659-9525; www.galantevineyards.com.

As the beach continues southward, its name changes to **Middle Beach**—a notoriously dangerous place to swim or sometimes even to walk, due to unpredictable high waves— and then **San Jose Beach**, more commonly known as Monastery Beach because it runs below the **Carmelite Monastery**. The Carmel River (and thus Carmel itself) got its name at the urging of three priests of the Carmelite order who accompanied explorer Juan Gaspar de Portolá on his 1769 expedition to the Monterey Peninsula and celebrated the first Catholic mass in central California at the mouth of the river. The first Carmelite monastery of nuns on the West Coast was established in Carmel in the 1920s. The present monastery, a graceful white structure with castlelike crenelated walls and a tall, slender bell tower, was built in the 1930s by Noel Sullivan, a former World War I ambulance company officer upon whom Ernest Hemingway based his protagonist in *A Farewell to Arms*; Sullivan's tomb is in the monastery. Today, about two dozen nuns live in the monastery under a vow of silence and only use their voices to sing mass. Visitors are welcome at morning mass and in the garden courtyard. ~ Route 1, one and a half miles south of Carmel-by-the-Sea.

History, classic Old World architecture and faith merge at **Carmel Mission Basilica**, the site of a Baroque Moorish–style mission built by Father Junipero Serra in 1770 as the center of

The padres kitchen at Carmel Mission.

a busy community in which 4000 Indians lived and thousands more came to work and worship. After Mexico won its independence from Spain in the 1820s, church property was secularized and the mission was abandoned and fell into such disrepair that little of the original building remains. Still, the 1930s reconstruction visitors see on the site today seems to glow with a patina of great age. Birds and flowers fill the courtyards. Three museum galleries exhibit Spanish colonial church artifacts and the first library in California. Visitors can also see a reconstruction of Father Serra's ascetic sleeping cell. Serra himself is buried in the sanctuary, his tomb marked with a stone plaque. Several thousand "mission Indians" are buried in the cemetery behind the church.

The basilica itself has a vaulted ceiling and lime plaster walls made from burned seashells and bedecked with colonial religious paintings and wood Christ fig-

OPPOSITE: Carmel Mission.

ures. ~ 3080 Rio Road; 831-624-1271; www.carmelmission.org.

Two miles south of Carmel-by-the-Sea stands **Point Lobos State Reserve**, a magnificent outcropping of granite headlands and secluded coves that once served as a whaling station and abalone cannery. The point itself was given to the state in the 1930s to protect it from development as the population of the Carmel area boomed. Over the years, the original 456 acres have been expanded to encompass 1225 acres—two-thirds of it underwater. There are many miles of hiking trails as well as picnic areas and restrooms. The Whalers Cabin and adjacent Whaling Station house a museum with exhibits about Point Lobos history and the 19th-century whaling industry. No dogs. Admission. ~ Route 1, three miles south of Carmel-by-the-Sea; 831-624-4909; pt-lobos.parks.state.ca.us, e-mail ptlobos@mbay.net.

outdoor adventures

HIKING

All distances listed for hiking trails are one-way unless otherwise noted.

Along 17 Mile Drive, you'll find two pretty nature trails that start at the Inn at Spanish Bay and together form a figure-8 loop around the golf course and down to Moss Beach. The 1.3-mile **Links Nature Walk** follows boardwalks across sand dunes from the cypress forest down along the beach and back to the inn, circling the north half of the property. The 1-mile **Bay Nature Walk** follows a similar woods, dunes and beach circuit around the south half of the inn grounds, with a picnic area along the way. Both trails are open to the general public. You can follow the beach southward from the Bay Nature Walk for a short distance to join the Point Joe to Bird Rock Trail below.

A little farther south along 17 Mile Drive, a 1.7-mile hiking trail follows the rim of the coastal shelf from the parking area at **Point Joe** to **Bird Rock**, offering exceptional sea views from rock promontories, good whale watching in migration season and eyefuls of seabird and seal colonies. Black-tailed deer are abundant in the area, and the wildflower displays in spring and early summer are incomparable. At the Bird Rock end of the trail, the 1-mile **Indian Village Trail** crosses the sand dunes and loops inland to the site of a pre-Columbian village that once stood near a sacred spring. No trace remains of the indigenous settlement; a picnic area now occupies the site.

Also in Pebble Beach, the **Samuel F.B. Morse Botanical Reserve** has 86 acres of diverse natural forest ranging from redwood stands to pygmy Gowen cypress (a species unique to Pebble Beach), along with pine, oak, ferns and vines. A 1.8-mile loop trail climbs up the slope of Huckleberry Hill before descending into a lush canyon. To reach the reserve and trailhead, follow the inland Pebble Beach tour route north from 17 Mile Drive's Highway One Gate to the intersection of Lopez Road and Congress Road, just past the Poppy Hills Golf Course. Turn right and drive to the reserve's parking area at the junction of Congress and Bird Rock roads.

A local secret on the edge of Carmel-by-the-Sea, **Mission Trails Park** has a 5-mile network of trails that wanders through 35 acres of lush canyon and wooded hillsides. Five interlocking trails run generally parallel to one another through the long, narrow park, inviting you to design your own route. While exploring, climb the **Flanders Trail** to view the exterior of the Flanders Mansion, a 1924 estate now owned by the village of

If you have time for just one hike in the Carmel area, try the breathtaking **North Shore Trail** at Point Lobos State Reserve, where you'll find seabird colonies, wind-twisted cypress trees, sheer granite cliffs, crashing surf and a historic cabin built by Chinese whalers.

Carmel-by-the-Sea, and explore its lovely one-acre native-plants garden. The main park trailhead is at the parking area near the intersection of Rio Road and Serra Trail, across from the Carmel Mission Basilica. There are also unmarked pedestrian entrances to the trail system at the east end of 11th Avenue and the corner of Mountain View and Crespi avenues. Dogs on leash are allowed in the park but not in the Flanders garden.

A 1-mile nature trail with interpretive signs leads from the **Carmel River Lagoon and Wetlands** parking area at Scenic Road and Carmelo Street along the edge of the protected wetlands and across the sandbar that separates the river mouth from the bay most of the time. The trail leads to a hilltop where a large wooden cross commemorates the landing of the 1769 Portolá-Crespi expedition. A trail continues south from the cross along the grassy bluffs above Carmel River State Beach, while another trail from the bottom of the hill follows the beach itself. The two trails join after three-fourths of a mile at the north end of Monastery Beach (San Jose Beach) and continue for another three-fourths of a mile to join the Point Lobos trail system at Ichxenta Point.

The ultimate hiking area around Carmel, **Point Lobos State Reserve** has 456 acres of land honeycombed with mostly level trails that wind through Monterey pine forests and along rocky cliffs overlooking sea lion coves and bird colonies. Literary luminaries including Robert Louis Stevenson and John Steinbeck used to draw inspiration from their frequent hikes here. Thirteen interconnecting trails cover a total distance of more than 26 miles, making for nearly endless mix-and-match hiking options. The .8-mile **Cypress Grove Trail**, leading through one of the last natural stands of Monterey cypress trees on the peninsula to cliff-top ocean vistas, is one of the most popular trails in the park. The .7-mile **Sea Lion Point Trail** loops along a coastal bluff overlooking a rocky cove that is home to sea otters, sea lions and harbor seals. The .8-mile **Bird Island Trail** leads to the white sands at China Cove and Gibson Beach, overlooking an island habitat for cormorants and brown pelicans. The .7-mile **Pine Ridge Trail** leads inland through pine and oak

Bird Rock.

forests teeming with birds, squirrels and deer. Longer hikes include the 1.4-mile **North Shore Trail** along the rocky headlands overlooking Cypress Cove, Guillemot Island with its seabird nesting area, Bluefish Cove and Whalers Cove. A complete
loop around the point via the North Shore Trail, the **South
Shore Trail** and the inland **Carmelo Meadows** and **South Pla-
teau trails** covers about five miles and takes half a day. Bikes
are allowed, but no dogs.

In the Carmel Valley, **Garland Ranch Regional Park** sprawls
across 4400 acres of the most varied terrain imaginable, from
redwood groves along the Carmel River up oaken canyons and
chaparral hillsides to the rugged Santa Lucia Mountains. A
spectacular web of more than a dozen interconnecting trails
meanders through forest, foothills and mountains, starting
from the visitors center on Carmel Valley Road. For an easy
wildflower hike, try the 1.4-mile **Lupine Loop Trail** from the
visitors center. From the same starting point, the **Buckeye
Nature Trail** leads through cool, damp forest lush with ferns
and mushrooms, with interpretive signs identifying plants and
explaining how they were used by local Indians; return via the
Cottonwood Trail for a 2-mile loop hike. For a longer trip,
turn off the Lupine Loop Trail on the **Waterfall Trail**, leading to Garland Ranch Falls, a cascade that plunges 70 feet into
a fern canyon, and then follow the **Mesa Trail** past pretty La
Mesa Pond to return to the Lupine Loop—a 3.5- to 4-mile cir-
cle that involves 600 feet of climbing. Or extend this hike with

an added 4-mile loop that follows the **Garzas Canyon Trail** from La Mesa Pond, then follows the **Snivley's Ridge Trail** on a steep ascent to a vista point 1600 feet up on the side of Pinyon Peak, and descends back to the pond along the switchback **Sky Trail**. Restrictions vary for different trails. Equestrians are allowed on some longer trails on the south side of the park but prohibited from most on the north side. Bikes are allowed only in a limited area at the northwest corner of the park behind the visitors center. Dogs are allowed on leash or under immediate voice control of their owners. Admission. ~ The park's main entrance is on Carmel Valley Road, 8.5 miles east of Route 1.

BIKING

Mountain bikes are allowed at **Point Lobos State Reserve** and in the Cooper Ranch area at the northwest corner of **Garland Ranch Regional Park** near the visitors center. See "Hiking" above for trail details.

The Carmel area offers excellent opportunities for on-road cycle touring. Foremost among them, **Carmel Valley Road** (Route G16) starts from Route 1 just north of the intersection with Rio Road and wanders through too-good-to-be-true rural landscapes for 12 miles to Garland Ranch Regional Park and the tiny commercial center of Carmel Valley Village, then con-

Biking along 17 Mile Drive.

tinues on an increasingly steep and winding course along the Carmel River for another 30 miles or so to unpaved Arroyo Seco Road, which climbs into the mountains of Los Padres National Forest.

17 Mile Drive also makes for a relaxing road ride, especially since the toll charge keeps the traffic light on all but the busiest weekends. Bicyclists are exempt from the toll.

Bicycle rentals are available at **Bay Bikes**. ~ 10 East Carmel Valley Road, Carmel Valley; 831-659-2453. **Carmel Bicycle** provides bike sales, service and route information, but not rentals. ~ Valley Hills Center, Carmel; 831-625-2211.

GOLF

The name Pebble Beach has been synonymous with golf for nearly a century, ever since 1913, when the community's developer, Samuel F. B. Morse, commissioned former California State Amateur champion Jack Neville to design a course "of unsurpassed scenic beauty with an element of difficulty that will always be challenged but never conquered." The result was the 6737-yard, par-72 **Pebble Beach Golf Links**, America's best-known golf course. The California State Amateur Golf Tournament was moved to Pebble Beach from Monterey's Del Monte Golf course in 1920 and has been played there ever since. The course has hosted the U.S. Amateur Golf Tournament and the U.S. Open Golf Tournament more often than any other golf course (four times each) and *Golf Digest* ranks it the third-best course in America, as well as the number-one resort course. Simply driving past it on 17 Mile Drive will show you why playing Pebble Beach, with its stage-like raised teeing area, always surrounded by onlooking lodge

IS THERE A TIGER IN YOUR WOOD?

If you have the time and wherewithal to play just one golf course on the Monterey Peninsula, why not make it the **Pebble Beach Golf Links**? Sure, the green fee is $275 plus cart rental and tee times can be booked solid for months in advance, but as once-in-a-lifetime experiences go, it's a bargain. The stage-style tee-off will make you feel like Tiger Woods, and from there the excitement just keeps on mounting.

Links at Spanish Bay.

guests, and spectacular seaside fairways, rollercoaster greens and giant bunkers, is many golf enthusiasts' lifelong dream. Reservations are required a day in advance for non-resort guests, though during the summer you'll want to apply weeks in advance if you hope to get a tee time. ~ 17 Mile Drive, Pebble Beach; 831-625-8518, 800-654-9300; www.pebblebeach.com.

Also owned by the Pebble Beach Company, the 6821-yard, par-72 **Links at Spanish Bay** resort course was designed by Robert Trent Jones, Jr., with Tom Watson and Frank "Sandy" Tatum as America's foremost Scottish links-style course. Resort guests have tee-time priority. ~ 2700 17 Mile Drive, Pebble Beach; 831-647-7495, 800-654-9300; www.pebblebeach.com.

Spyglass Hill Golf Course enjoys a reputation as the toughest golf course in Northern California and one of the most difficult in the world. The first five holes of this 6862-yard, par-72 semi-private resort course operated by the Pebble Beach Company are set among spectacular sand dunes. Spyglass Hill hosts the AT&T Pebble Beach National Pro-Am Golf Tournament as well as the qualifying rounds for the California State Amateur Tournament. ~ Stevenson Drive at Spyglass Hill Road, Pebble Beach; 831-625-8563, 800-654-9300; www.pebblebeach.com.

The 6861-yard, par-72 **Poppy Hills Golf Course**, designed by Robert Trent Jones in 1986, is known for its vast undulating greens, guarded bunkers and pot bunkers. ~ 3200 Lopez Road, Pebble Beach; 831-625-2154; www.poppyhillsgolf.com.

In Carmel Valley, the public **Rancho Canada Golf Club** has 36 holes—a 6109-yard, par-71 east course and a 6349-yard, par-72 west course. Both feature short, tight fairways with lots of trees at the foot of the Santa Lucia Mountains. The Carmel River meanders through the courses, providing a long, sometimes tricky water hazard. ~ 4860 Carmel Valley Road, Carmel Valley; 831-624-0111; www.ranchocanada.com.

Two private resorts in the Carmel Valley are also open to nonguests on a limited basis. The **Golf Course at Quail Lodge** features fast greens, challenging sand and water hazards, and inspiring mountain views. ~ 8000 Valley Green Drive, Carmel; 831-624-2779, fax 831-629-8481; www.quaillodge.com. The **Carmel Valley Ranch Resort** has a course designed by Peter Dye with wide greens, bunkers bordered with railroad ties, and a tough, hilly back nine. ~ 1 Old Ranch Road, Carmel Valley; 831-626-2510, 800-422-7635, fax 831-626-2532.

TENNIS

You'll find 18 clay courts and instruction programs for all skill levels at the **Carmel Valley Racquet Club**. Visitors pay a fee to use facilities. Reservations required. ~ 27300 Rancho San Carlos Road, Carmel Valley; 831-624-2737.

Serious tennis enthusiasts may want to consider a stay at **John Gardiner's Tennis Ranch**, one of the world's most prestigious tennis resorts. The resort features ten championship courts and two teaching courts, as well as three swimming pools, a fitness center and a spa. Open only to club members and resort guests. ~ 114 Carmel Valley Road, Carmel Valley; 831-659-2207, 800-453-6225; www.tennis-ranch.com.

DIVING

Scuba divers find the 80-foot-high kelp forests offshore at **Point Lobos State Reserve** to be one of the most

fascinating dive sites on the California coast. Lingcod, rock-fish and cabezone abound. Reservations are required and can be made up to two months in advance by phone or e-mail. ~ Route 1, three miles south of Carmel-by-the-Sea; 831-624-4909; pt-lobos.parks.state.ca.us, e-mail ptlobos@mbay.net.

The closest dive shops are in Monterey (see Chapter 4).

RIDING STABLES

Guided private and group trail rides along the dunes and beach or through the cypress forest are available at the **Pebble Beach Equestrian Center**. Reservations required. ~ Portola Road at Alva Lane, Pebble Beach; 831-624-2756; www.ridepebblebeach.com.

For a horseback ride in 400 acres of hills and meadows in the Carmel Valley, visit **Holman Ranch**. ~ Mile 12.5, Carmel Valley Road; 831-659-6054; www.holmanranch.com.

CAMPING

None of the large state parks and reserves around Carmel have camping facilities. There are two adja-

Carmel Valley.

cent private campgrounds in Carmel Valley, both at the end of Schulte Road, which turns off to the right four and a half miles up Carmel Valley Road. **Saddle Mountain Recreation Park** has 25 tent sites and 25 RV sites with full hookups in an oak grove by the river. All sites have picnic tables, food lockers and barbecue grills; campground facilities include restrooms with showers. Sites cost $25 to $40 per night, first-come, first-served on weeknights. Open year-round. ~ Schulte Road, Carmel Valley; 831-624-1617, fax 831-624-4470.

Nearby, **Carmel by the River RV Park** has 35 luxury RV sites with full hookups including cable TV and computer modems and flower-garden privacy hedges. The campground has restrooms with showers. Sites cost $40 to $45 per night. Reservations accepted for stays of two nights or longer. Open year-round. ~ Schulte Road, Carmel Valley; 831-624-9329, fax 831-624-8416. The parks share recreational facilities including basketball and volleyball courts, a game room and a river beach; a grocery store is located nearby.

An Ocean Avenue landmark, the **La Playa Hotel** grew from a mansion designed in 1904 by artist Christopher Jorgensen for his bride, a member of the Ghirardelli family of San Francisco choco-

Lodging

late makers. Since Jorgensen is best known for his romantic paintings of California missions, it's only natural that the architecture of the stone residence should reflect the Mission Revival style in vogue at the time. After part of the house was destroyed by fire in the 1920s, it was reconstructed from the original floor plans and expanded into a luxury hotel. Today, following a multimillion-dollar makeover in the 1980s and the addition of a modern annex, the La Playa has become a four-story (no elevator), 80-unit resort with ocean views, heated pool, full-service spa and a restaurant overlooking carefully manicured formal gardens. Some rooms have kitchens. The beach is just two blocks away. ~ Camino Real at 8th Avenue, Carmel-by-the-Sea; 831-624-6476, 800-582-8900, fax 831-624-7966; www.laplayahotel.com, e-mail tglidden@laplayahotel.com. DELUXE TO ULTRA-DELUXE.

Reasonable rates (for Carmel, that is) are among the virtues at **Svendsgaard's Inn**, a low-slung complex built around a garden courtyard, lawn and swimming pool and surrounded by

The Hotel That Gave Birth to Carmel

Carmel-by-the-Sea's most historic hotel, the **Pine Inn** was built by Frank Devendorf, the San Jose real estate broker who later created Carmel-by-the-Sea, in 1889. The lobby gleams with polished hardwood wall paneling, a fireplace and antique chandeliers, oriental rugs and Chinese furnishings in black lacquer trimmed in gold leaf with red upholstery. The melding of Victorian and Asian styles carries over into the 49 guest rooms. Though the less-expensive rooms are small (as hotel rooms of the period tended to be), all rooms have canopied beds, private baths, televisions and telephones. This elegant little hotel has a restaurant and bar downstairs and offers room service. ~ Ocean Avenue at Monte Verde Street, Carmel-by-the-Sea; 831-624-3851, 800-228-3851, fax 831-624-3030; www.pine-inn.com, e-mail info@pine-inn.com. DELUXE TO ULTRA-DELUXE.

••

The Zen of Hot Water

Hidden away on a long, winding side road off upper Carmel Valley Road, about as deep in the forest as you can get by car, the legendary **Tassajara Zen Mountain Center** offers simple accommodations, campsites and vegetarian meals. No phones, telephones or other electronics are provided or allowed, and to get there you must walk in from a distant parking area. Hot springs, believed to have been revered by American Indians for their curative powers, feed private pools and a large swimming pool (bathing suits required at all pools). The center is operated by the San Francisco Zen Center, the first Soto Zen monastery outside Asia. Open to the public May to early September. ~ Tassajara Road, Los Padres National Forest; contact San Francisco Zen Center, 300 Page Street, San Francisco; 415-865-1895, reservations (April 1 to September 1) 415-865-1899; www.sfzc.com.

••

pines. The 34 guest rooms and suites, though generally motel-like, are spacious and bright, and many feature king-size beds, fireplaces, kitchenettes, microwaves and two-person jacuzzi tubs. Breakfast and the morning paper are delivered to your door. Room rates drop into the moderate range from November through June. ~ 4th Avenue at San Carlos Street, Carmel-by-the-Sea; 831-624-1511, 800-433-4732, fax 831-624-5661; www.svendsgaardsinn.com, e-mail svendsgaards@innsbythesea.com. DELUXE TO ULTRA-DELUXE.

On the southern outskirts of town, the **Carmel River Inn** offers both large motel-style rooms and more appealing wood-frame cottages. The less-expensive guest rooms have warm,

Mission Ranch Resort.

Highlands Inn—Park Hyatt Carmel.

though uninspired, decor along with wall-to-wall carpeting, refrigerators, phones and televisions. The cottages are attractive
one- and two-bedroom units, some with kitchens and fireplaces.
Several decks surround a heated outdoor pool. ~ Route 1 at
Carmel River Bridge, Carmel; 831-624-1575, 800-882-8124, fax
831-624-0290; www.carmelriverinn.com, e-mail info@carmel
riverinn.com. MODERATE TO ULTRA-DELUXE.

A local secret in an ideal setting near Carmel Mission
Basilica, Mission Trails Park and Carmel River State Beach,
Mission Ranch Resort overlooks the river with a dramatic view
of Point Lobos and the Santa Lucia Mountains. The 31 comfortable guest units are in three-plex and four-plex cottages and
a white-clapboard farmhouse-style main lodge surrounded by
ancient cypress trees. The 22 acres of grounds surround six
championship tennis courts, a fitness facility and a dining
room. Rates include continental breakfast. ~ 26270 Dolores
Street, Carmel; 831-624-6436, 800-538-8221, fax 831-626-4163.
MODERATE TO ULTRA-DELUXE.

Set on rocky bluffs above the coastline in the exclusive residential area of Carmel Highlands, just south of Point Lobos, the **Highlands Inn—Park Hyatt Carmel** sets the standard in contemporary luxury with its stone lodge and surrounding wood-shingle buildings. Each of the 142 spacious guest suites has separate bedroom and living room areas with modern blonde-wood decor, a fireplace and an ocean-view patio or balcony; some have private spas. For visitors who crave the ultimate in out-of-town California-chic accommodations, this is it. ~ Route 1, four miles south of Carmel; 831-620-1234, 800-682-4811, fax 831-626-1574; www.highlands-inn.com. ULTRA-DELUXE.

dining
• • • • • • • • • • • • • •

The **Tuck Box**, a gingerbread-style building with a swirly roof and a curved chimney, is the perpetually "in" place to come for afternoon tea. The prim little dining room, which feels a little like being in a huge Victorian dollhouse, serves breakfast and lunch as well. The lunch menu features omelettes, sandwiches, shrimp salad and Welsh rarebit. Tea comes with scones, muffins or other homemade baked goods. ~ Dolores Street between Ocean and 7th avenues, Carmel-by-the-Sea; 831-624-6365, fax 831-626-3939; www.tuckbox.com. BUDGET TO MODERATE.

Food and wine critics are unanimous in their assessment of **Anton & Michel** as the ultimate dining experience in Carmel-by-the-Sea. Established in 1980, the restaurant overlooks the Court of the Fountains just off Ocean Avenue. The restaurant focuses on exceptional presentations of classic Continental cuisine including appetizers such as escargot and salmon gravlax; luncheon choices such as local petrale sole and chicken Jerusalem; dinner entrées that include rack of lamb or chateaubriand for two, Monterey Bay abalone and tenderloin steak *au poivre flambé*; and a selection of desserts like cherries jubilee, bananas Foster, tiramisu and crème brûlée—and, of course, an impeccable wine list. The stage is set by warm pastel and earth-tone decor with a country French flair and fine-quality original oil paintings. ~ Mission Street between Ocean and 7th

avenues, Carmel-by-the-Sea; 831-624-2406, fax 831-625-1542; www.carmelsbest.com/antonmichel.

There's likely to be a line waiting in front of **Tutto Mondo's Trattoria**, and the wait is worth it. Step through the front door,

and suddenly you're in Italy, wrapped in an Old World ambience of wine bottles, garlic strings and cooking utensils that double as decor. The staff has been known to burst into song—and you may, too, as you dig into a heaping plate of one of the restaurant's authentic pasta dishes such as *la mafiosa* (calamari, prawns and scallops in a spicy tomato sauce). There are also changing dinner specials featuring veal, chicken, seafood and fish. Save room for the tiramisu. ~ Dolores Street Between Ocean and 7th Avenues, Carmel-by-the-Sea; 831-624-

Tutto Mondo's Trattoria.

8977, fax 831-624-4102; www.mondos.com, e-mail info@mon dos.com. MODERATE TO DELUXE.

A rarity in Carmel, the **Rio Grill** is reasonably priced as well as critically acclaimed. The food at this casual, contemporary café is all-American with a Southwestern flair. Try the smoked chicken with artichokes or the calf's liver with sweet potato pancake. ~ Crossroads Shopping Center, Route 1 at Rio Road, Carmel; 831-625-5436, fax 831-625-2950; www.rio grill.com, e-mail will@riogrill.com. MODERATE TO DELUXE.

For those with champagne-and-escargot taste but a burgers-and-beer budget, the place to go is **Patisserie Boissière**, a simple French country–style restaurant adjoining a small bakery. Besides fantastic pastries for breakfast (or just about anytime), there's lunch daily, dinner Wednesday through Sunday, and brunch on the weekends. The menu features such entrées as coquilles St. Jacques, braised lamb shank and parchment-cooked salmon. No dinner Mondays and Tuesdays. ~ Carmel

Plaza, Mission Street between Ocean and 7th avenues, Carmel; 831-624-5008, fax 831-626-9155. MODERATE.

Locals have been dining out at the **Restaurant at Mission Ranch** since the days when it was a creamery, back when Carmel-by-the-Sea was barely a gleam in its founder's eye. The cows are gone—replaced by a decorative scattering of sheep—and the building is homier than ever with its stone fireplace and ocean view. The menu, too, is tried-and-true—fresh seafood, steak, prime rib, chicken and pasta.

Restaurant at Mission Ranch.

There's dinner nightly, lunch on Saturday, and brunch on Sunday. ~ 26270 Dolores Street, Carmel; 831-625-9040, fax 831-625-5502. MODERATE TO ULTRA-DELUXE.

Feeding and reading go hand-in-hand at the **Thunderbird Bookshop and Café**, an outstanding independent bookstore with indoor and outdoor dining areas. Lunch is served all day, with light fare that includes soups, salads and pot pies as well as a tasty selection of desserts. ~ 3600 The Barnyard, Carmel Valley; 831-624-1803; www.thunderbirdbooks.com, e-mail info@thunderbirdbooks.com. BUDGET.

Dancing and live music are prohibited by local ordinance in Carmel-by-the-Sea, but what the village may lack in terms of a club scene is more than compensated for by the abundance of cul-

nightlife

tural offerings. Founded in 1901, the **Forest Theatre** is surrounded by trees, with two large fire pits alongside and Point Lobos as a backdrop. In the summer and fall the theater offers a variety of stage presentations and festivals, culminating in the annual Carmel Shakespeare Festival. ~ Mountain View Ave-

••
Dining with Dirty Harry

Sure, it's touristy. On summer weekends you can wait hours for a table. And the multitude of beef entrées named after Dirty Harry makes the menu seem almost kitsch. But let's face it, who can resist telling the folks back home about dining at the **Hog's Breath Inn**, the first restaurant established by Carmel's former mayor and most celebrated living resident, actor Clint Eastwood? The inn has weathered wood beams, fireplaces and an Old West atmosphere, not to mention mounted hog heads on the walls and plenty of portraits of Eastwood. Besides the Dirty Harry Bacon Cheeseburger, luncheon choices include a wild turkey burger and vegetable lasagna. There's also a Dirty Harry Dinner (chopped sirloin with wild mushrooms and garlic "smashed" potatoes) as well as a full range of California cuisine from Humongous Fungus (a portobello mushroom marinated in wine, herbs and garlic and served with marsala sauce) to seared ahi tuna crusted with sesame seeds and cracked peppercorn. Castroville artichoke soup is a specialty. ~ San Carlos Street between 5th and 6th avenues, Carmel-by-the-Sea; 831-625-1044, fax 831-625-2188; www.hogsbreathinn.net. MODERATE TO DELUXE.
••

nue and Santa Rita Street, Carmel-by-the-Sea; 831-626-1681, fax 831-626-0772.

Another historic theater, the **Golden Bough Playhouse** was originally established in 1907. It burned down in 1935 during a production of *By Candlelight* and was rebuilt in a new location where it once again burned down while staging—yes—*By Candlelight* again. Rebuilt in 1950, the theater presents performances of contemporary plays (but not *By Candlelight)* by the Pacific Repertory Theatre. ~ Monte Verde Street between 8th and 9th avenues, Carmel-by-the-Sea; 831-622-0700; www.pacrep.org.

The **Indoor Forest Theatre** (831-624-1531) and the **Carl Cherry Foundation** (831-624-7491), the former home of inventor Carl Cherry, also present performances by a variety of local arts organizations including the **Carmel Bach Festival** (831-624-1521; www.backfestival.org), the **California Performing Arts Festival** (831-624-7675; www.carmelfest.org), the **Children's Experimental Theatre** (831-624-1531) and the **Monterey County Symphony Association** (831-624-8511, 800-698-1138; www.montereysymphony.org).

If drinks and live music are a must in your vacation itinerary, your best bet may be the **Lobos Lounge** at Highlands Inn. With a piano bar during the week and a jazz trio on weekends, this may not exactly be the kind of place where you want to boogie 'til you can't boogie no more, but the wild Point Lobos coastline through the plate-glass wall is an incomparable view for sipping cocktails. ~ Route 1, four miles south of Carmel; 831-620-1234, fax 831-626-1574; www.highlands-inn.com.

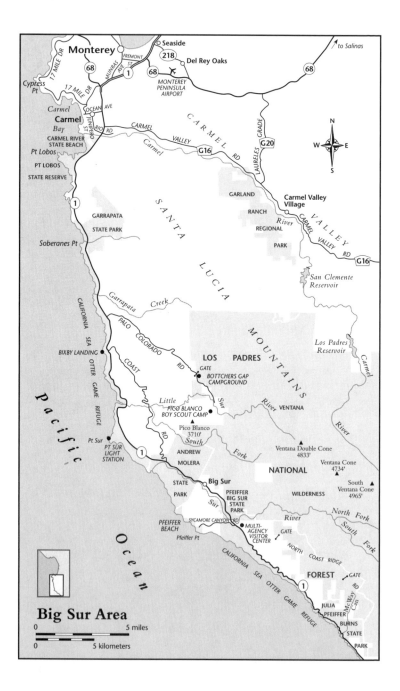

to Salinas

Monterey
Seaside
218
Del Rey Oaks
68
FREMONT
MUNRAS AVE ST
1
68
17 MILE DR
Cypress Pt
17 MILE DR
MONTEREY
PENINSULA
AIRPORT
C A R M E L
68
LAURELES GRADE
OCEAN AVE
Carmel
Carmel
JUNIPERO ST
RIO RD
CARMEL
Bay
CARMEL
VALLEY
Carmel
G16
RD
G20
CARMEL RIVER
STATE BEACH
Pt Lobos
PT LOBOS
STATE RESERVE
GARLAND
V A L L E Y
**Carmel Valley
Village**
RANCH
River
CARMEL
1
GARRAPATA
STATE PARK
S A N T A
REGIONAL
VALLEY
G16
PARK
RD
Soberanes Pt
*San Clemente
Reservoir*
L U C I A
Garrapata
Creek
CALIFORNIA SEA
PALO
M O U N T A I N S
*Los Padres
Reservoir*
Carmel
BIXBY LANDING
COLORADO
OTTER GAME REFUGE
COAST
LOS PADRES
GATE
BOTTCHERS GAP
CAMPGROUND
RD
P a c i f i c
Little
PICO BLANCO
BOY SCOUT CAMP
Sur
River
VENTANA
River
▲ Pico Blanco
3710'
Pt Sur
RD
South
PT SUR
LIGHT
STATION
ANDREW
Fork
Ventana Double Cone
4833' ▲
1
MOLERA
NATIONAL
Ventana Cone
4734' ▲
STATE
Big Sur
PARK
PFEIFFER
BIG SUR
STATE
PARK
WILDERNESS
South
Ventana Cone
4965' ▲
Sur
PFEIFFER
BEACH
SYCAMORE CANYON RD
River
North Fork
Pfeiffer Pt
MULTI-
AGENCY
VISITOR
CENTER
GATE
NORTH
COAST
RIDGE
South Fork
O c e a n
CALIFORNIA SEA
FOREST
GATE
RD
OTTER
GAME
1
McWay Can
JULIA
REFUGE
PFEIFFER
BURNS
STATE
PARK

Big Sur Area
0   5 miles
0   5 kilometers

6

Big Sur

The Spanish colonists who originally settled the Monterey Peninsula called the wilderness to the south *El País Grande del Sur* ("The Big Land to the South") but never explored it. The sheer cliffs rising up out of the water for hundreds of feet made the area unapproachable by sea. The steep Santa Lucia Mountains, sliced by a series of deep gorges running parallel to the coast, made it unreachable by land. Through two centuries of Spanish, Mexican and U.S. occupation, as explorers blazed wagon-train and stagecoach routes across the scorching desert of Death Valley and prospectors panned every stream in the High Sierra, Big Sur remained terra incognita.

It was only in the late 19th century that the government encouraged settlers to homestead in Big Sur Valley.

Anyone willing to commit to the challenges of building a life in the wild, redwood-shrouded landscape could buy 160 acres along the Big Sur River for a mere $200. The problem—and the reason no sizeable community was ever built there—was that Big Sur remained as inaccessible as ever by either land or sea. Would-be pioneers' possessions were limited to what they could carry on muleback through the dense coastal forests and up and down the slippery slopes of the Santa Lucia Mountains, which no road crosses even today, and those they could fashion from local wood and stone. In an area unsuited to farming and beyond the reach of any store, food supplies could only come from hunting, fishing or foraging. Well into the 20th century, Big Sur remained one of the last unexplored places in California, as primitive a wilderness as any on earth.

It was not until 1938 that Big Sur became accessible to visitors, thanks to the ambitious road-building project that resulted in Route 1. The road took 17 years to complete. It required

construction of 32 bridges across once-uncrossable gorges, braving obstacles that included high winds, fog and landslides.

When Route 1 finally opened, the Big Sur Valley soon blossomed into an artists' and

Sea lions sunning in Point Lobos.

writers' colony, but one with a far different character than Carmel-by-the-Sea. Instead of a compact, rectangular village of cute little fairytale cottages, Big Sur became a place of rustic cabins hewn from locally cut logs, thinly scattered up a few long, winding roads so that a person living in one cabin might walk a good distance before catching sight of another. This kind of isolation appealed especially to unconventional writers who sought to keep their distance from the mainstream American culture of the 1950s and '60s. It was no accident that the name Big Sur came to be identified with such authors as Jack Kerouac, Henry Miller and Richard Brautigan.

Today Big Sur's artistic and literary counterculture, like that of Carmel, has largely been displaced by skyrocketing prices for the limited amount of real estate that is under private ownership. Yet at places such as the secluded Esalen Institute conference center, cultural creativity continues to evolve in new, 21st-century ways. Meanwhile, each year more motorists drive the most spectacular stretch of Route 1 for the pure fun of it. Many Big Sur residents complain about the steady flow of day-trippers. In fact, during the 1980s, locals seriously proposed barricading the highway to restore Big Sur's past peace and quiet. When mudslides closed the highway for more than a year, however, people in Big Sur experienced the true meaning of wilderness life. Tourism revenues teetered on the brink of collapse, and folks began to appreciate the virtue of being able to drive into Monterey for supplies once in a while.

••
Driving on the Edge

There are stone walls on some curves along Route 1 to keep the incautious from careening over the side. Elsewhere there are metal guard rails. As often as not, there is only an unprotected dropoff, tribute to the relatively recent discovery that fewer accidents happen when there are no guard rails to provide reckless drivers with a false sense of confidence.

Many pullouts offer scenic vistas of the shoreline that lies too directly below to be seen from the road. Pleasure travelers will find themselves taking advantage of these pullouts frequently, whether or not they really want to take in the view, because the scariest thing about driving this and other two-lane segments of Route 1 is not the steep dropoffs—it's locals who drive the highway regularly, know it like the backs of their hands and rudely flash their lights or honk their horns if you obstruct their progress by failing to maintain an absolutely insane speed. It's true, you can drive from Carmel to the Big Sur Visitors Center in a mere 20 minutes if you keep the speedometer needle on 80—or in more than two hours if you stop to take in the scenery every chance you get.

••

Unlike the Monterey Bay area, Big Sur hasn't developed much in the way of commercial sporting activities. You won't find any golf courses here, nor dive or surf shops. Few lodges in the area even have swimming pools. What you will find is a boundless natural setting for hiking both in the expansive state parks along Route 1 and in the vast 216,500-acre Ventana Wilderness, which spans most of the Santa Lucia range, as wild today as it was when the first pioneers ventured into it a century or so ago. Here you can stroll through redwood groves or along rocky headlands for an hour, or you can

trek for 80 miles through rugged mountains
without ever crossing a road.

As you head south from Point Lobos along
Route 1, the gateway to Big Sur country an-
nounces itself without a touch of subtlety.
The highway seems to be heading on a col-

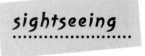

sightseeing

lision course with a solid wall of near-vertical mountain slopes,
only to veer seaward at the last possible moment. From there,
southbound motorists find themselves literally on edge for the
next 20 miles as the road traverses sea cliffs as much as 300
feet above the crashing surf.

Seven miles south of Carmel you'll come to the first of several wonderful state parks along the route. Wide and sugar-
white, the beach at **Garrapata State Park** is a clothing-optional
local favorite. There are no facilities—and no lifeguards, ei-

Bixby Creek Bridge.

ther. Treacherous currents make swimming a dangerous notion. From dramatic Soberanes Point, the park boundaries extend a good distance inland, to narrow, moist fern canyons and ancient redwood stands. ~ Route 1, just north of Garrapata Creek Bridge; 831-667-2315.

To get a close-up look at the country that lies inland from the coast, take a side trip up **Palo Colorado Road** about two miles south of Garrapata Creek. The paved one-lane road pierces the sun-speckled darkness of the deep redwood forest, passing rustic cabins and country homes, for eight miles to the Los Padres National Forest boundary, where there is a public campground and a gate protecting the Pico Blanco Boy Scout Camp at road's end. Return to Route 1 the same way you came.

A couple of miles farther along Route 1 will bring you to **Bixby Landing**, the site of an early-day shipment point for redwood-forest products en route to San Francisco, and **Bixby Creek Bridge**. The 714-foot span arching 260 feet over a forbidding chasm was the last piece of Route 1 to be completed. Locals will still sometimes declare that it is the world's longest concrete arch—which it is not, but at the time it was built it *was* the longest such arch west of the Mississippi. It still may well be the prettiest.

Just before the Bixby Creek Bridge, another side road makes for a spectacular (and hair-raising) scenic detour. The **Coast Road**, which provided access to rustic resorts in the Big Sur area before Route 1 was completed, edges along canyon rims, switchbacks through deep forested gorges and climbs mountain ridges for unforgettable views. The drive—unpaved, rutted, narrow and slippery when wet—is equally unforgettable and only for the bold. After 11 miles, the old Coast Road comes out at Andrew Molera State Park. Route 1 will seem a lot less nerve-wracking once you've considered the alternative.

If you stick to Route 1, you'll ascend **Hurricane Point**, a rock promontory with a classic Big Sur view and, most likely, high winds. From there, the road eases back down close to sea level and provides access to **Little Sur Beach**, a curving strand alongside a shallow lagoon bounded by hills and sand dunes. Another long beach ends at the volcanic headland where **Point Sur Light Station** has stood since 1889. The lighthouse can only be seen on one of the guided tours that run Saturdays at 10 a.m. and 2 p.m. and Sundays at 10 a.m. Admission. ~ 831-625-4419.

Both beaches, as well as the rest of the coastline between Garrapata and Andrew Molera state parks, are under the ju-

risdiction of the **California Sea Otter Game Refuge**. From the beach at water level, especially with the aid of binoculars, you're almost certain to glimpse some of these frisky mammals, which, until recently, balanced precariously on the brink of extinction.

Two miles south of Point Sur, the three-mile-long beach at **Andrew Molera State Park** is just a small part of the 4800-acre park, which climbs nearly 3500 feet up the mountainsides through forest that ranges from riparian cottonwoods to oaks and redwoods and abounds with wildlife on both land and sea. The Big Sur River meanders through the park, flowing into the sea at its north end. There are restrooms but no other facilities. While some of the park's 15 miles of trails are suited only for foot travel, this is the only Big Sur park where mountain biking and horseback riding are allowed; a concessionaire rents horses on-site. Day-use fee. ~ Route 1; 831-667-2315, fax 831-667-2886.

First-time visitors are sometimes baffled to discover that there is no village at **Big Sur**, which appears on maps as a town with a population of approximately 1000. In fact, these 1000 hardy souls live in widely scattered homes and cabins along a six-mile stretch of river valley, punctuated here and there by a family-run store, restaurant or inn. From the point where it

Pfeiffer Big Sur State Park.

meets the Big Sur River in Andrew Molera State Park, Route 1 veers away from the ocean and follows the river all the way up the populated part of the valley. It passes through **Pfeiffer Big Sur State Park**, 800 acres of primeval redwood forest along the river's bank around its central attraction—**Pfeiffer Falls**, pouring through a dark, mysterious-looking fern canyon. The roadside part of the park almost seems more developed than the private property to the north and south, with a grocery store, a restaurant, a gift shop, a laundromat and guest cottages as well as picnic areas and restrooms with showers. A **Multi-Agency Visitor Center**, operated jointly by the U.S. Forest Service, the California Parks Department, and the California Fish and Game Department, has backcountry maps and can offer hiking advice. Although rangers assure visitors that wild salmon and trout abound in the river, fishing is prohibited. ~ Route 1, Big Sur; 831-667-2315, fax 831-667-2886.

BIG SUR ON THE RUN

As great as the hiking is around Big Sur, the area is at least as well-known for running. The **Big Sur Marathon**, which takes place in April, has been called the best marathon in North America by runners' magazines. For those who just can't get enough, a 5K marathon is held the same weekend. ~ 831-625-6226. Before the marathon was introduced, there was the **Big Sur River Run**, which has been held annually since 1980. Held in October, the race follows a scenic, level course through the redwoods. ~ 831-624-4112. Cross-country runners come from far and wide on New Year's Day for the **Rio Resolution Run**, a contest that takes place on a course laid out along back roads, trails and beaches. ~ 831-624-4112.

Just south of the visitors center and park boundary, Big Sur's real commercial area begins. Although it's miles from the official map location of the town of Big Sur, this cluster of inns, restaurants, art galleries and travelers' services has been the "real" Big Sur for a century—ever since Florence Pfeiffer decided to charge $3 a head for bed and breakfast at her husband's ranch, spawning the concept of Big Sur as a tourist destination, while the Pfeiffer men lobbied the legislature to build a highway that would enable visitors to reach it by passenger car.

Across the highway a short distance from the visitors center, unmarked Sycamore Canyon Road descends for two miles to **Pfeiffer Beach**. Don't miss it—it's the most beautiful beach south of Carmel, made more enchanting by the fact that it's

Henry Miller Memorial Library.

not only isolated but also secret. Boulders lie strewn around the beach like a giant game of marbles. A little creek flows out of a deep, narrow canyon and slices the beach in two as it reaches out for the sea. Waves crash against offshore rock formations sculpted by time and saltwater into arches. There are restrooms but no other facilities. Day-use fee, $5. ~ 831-667-2423.

You first catch sight of the ocean again as you reach the famed Nepenthe restaurant (see below). Watch for the sign nearby directing you to the **Henry Miller Memorial Library**.

Sculpture at Henry Miller Memorial Library.

The controversial author, a Big Sur local from 1947 to 1964, wrote several major novels here, not least of which was the one to which he gave the provocative title *Big Sur and the Oranges of Hieronymous Bosch*. The curator claims the library contains every word of Miller's published work; there are also an exhibit of his evocative paintings and drawings, and various editions of Miller novels for sale. Closed Mondays. ~ Route 1; 831-667-2574.

As you leave Big Sur Valley and return to the Pacific shoreline, you suddenly find yourself traversing dark granite cliffs even higher and steeper than before. The edgy, spectacular highway goes on for ten miles before reaching **Julia Pfeiffer Burns State Park**, a 3580-acre expanse that takes in both sides of the highway as it climbs from the ocean surf to an elevation of 1500 feet. The heart of the park is steep redwood-shrouded defile through which McWay Creek spills down to the surf. There are picnic areas and restrooms. ~ Route 1; 831-667-2315, fax 831-667-2886.

outdoor adventures

HIKING

All distances listed for hiking trails are one-way unless otherwise noted.

At **Garrapata State Park**, the 1.5-mile **Soberanes Canyon Trail** ascends through a lush canyon with fern grottos and redwood groves, making its way back and forth across Soberanes Creek on footbridges. The upper part of the trail involves a steep climb and descent to navigate around an especially narrow part of the canyon. For a longer hike, continue to the end of the canyon as the trail climbs to intersect the **Rocky Ridge Trail**, climbing an arid hillside to 1400 feet for spectacular sea, canyon and mountain views before following the ridgeline back down to the Soberanes Canyon trailhead. The two trails combine to make a six-mile loop.

If you take only one hike in the Big Sur area, make it the hike past **McWay Falls** and up the **Ewoldsen Trail**, a 4.5-mile lollipop loop that has everything—a canyon waterfall, redwoods, a climb that will get your blood racing and an astonishing clifftop view.

Another hiking trail on the seaward side of the highway loops around **Soberanes Point**, where 280-foot Whale Peak is a good whale-watching spot. The complete loop is a little over two miles in length, depending on whether you decide to scramble up to the summit of the hill.

Andrew Molera State Park has 11 hiking trails totaling more than 15 miles in length. The shorter ones follow various

routes from the parking area down to the shore at Molera Beach or the headlands at Molera Point. Trails follow both shores of the Big Sur River not only down to the shore but also up to the east park boundary, making a natural loop trip that crosses the river on footbridges. The loop to the shore and back via the **Beach Trail** and **Headlands Trail** covers about three miles; the trip upriver and back on the **River Trail** and **Bobcat Trail** is about five miles long. The two can be combined. An even more ambitious loop trip on the **Bluffs Trail**, **Panorama Trail** and **Ridge Trail** follows the edge of the bluffs for the length of the park's coastline with beach access along the way, then climbs more than 1000 feet before descending through redwood forest back to the trailhead, a total distance of nine miles.

Pfeiffer Big Sur State Park has a half-dozen trails of various lengths, most of which have different starting points and run in different directions. The main event is the **Mount Manuel Trail**, a 5.2-mile ascent to an overlook just below the top of the 3380-foot peak for the most spectacular panorama in the Big Sur area. Allow all day. A less ambitious way to sample the best of the park, the 2-mile **Pfeiffer Falls–Valley View Trail** starts near the park entrance gate and crosses seven footbridges to reach Pfeiffer Falls before struggling up a ridgeline to a 450-foot-high overlook then returning to the canyon floor and the trailhead.

The main trail in **Julia Pfeiffer Burns State Park**, the easy .75-mile jaunt to **McWay Falls**, continues up McWay Canyon to connect with the **Ewoldsen Trail**, a 3-mile loop that starts in the redwoods and climbs 1600 feet to a ridgeline with a pair of precarious vista points on the edge of a cliff high above the sea.

Filling much of Los Padres National Forest, the 216,500-acre **Ventana Wilderness** encompasses most of the incredibly rugged Santa Lucia Range, rising to altitudes of 5800 feet. The wilderness area has 237 miles of hiking trails through landscapes almost untouched by humans, where golden eagles soar and deer and turkeys play—not to mention mountain lions and wild boars. While most major trailheads are on the other side of the mountains (see "Tassajara Zen Mountain

Opposite: Garrapata State Beach.

Center" in Chapter 5), there are wilderness portals on the ocean side at **Bottchers Gap** on the Palo Colorado Road and near the **Multi-Agency Visitor Center** in Big Sur. The 4-mile **Bottchers Gap—Devils Peak Trail** climbs steep slopes through evergreen forests for panoramic views of the northern section of the wilderness. From Big Sur, the rigorous 41-mile **Pine Ridge Trail** crosses the wilderness west-to-east, with a series of backpackers' campgrounds along the way, finally reaching the end of the trail at China Camp on the road to Tassajara Zen Mountain Center. ~ 831-667-2315.

CAMPING

Set in a redwood canyon in the mountains just inside the **Los Padres National Forest** boundary, ten miles up a narrow paved road from Route 1, **Bottchers Gap Walk-in Campground** has 11 tent sites designed to serve backpackers as a gateway to the northern Ventana Wilderness. There are picnic tables and grills, and the campground has outhouses but no drinking water. Sites cost $12 per night, first-come, first-served. Open year-round. ~ Palo Colorado Road; 831-385-5434.

Another hikers' oasis, **Andrew Molera State Park**'s walk-in campground is little more than an open meadow that invites campers to pitch their tents wherever they want. It's 150 yards from the car parking area and one mile from the beach along a scenic trail. The campground has picnic tables, grills and out-houses; drinking water is available. Fee, $1 per person per night, first-come, first-served. Despite a three-day limit, campers can find their tents sandwiched in wall-to-wall at busy times. Open year-round. ~ Route 1; 831-667-2315, fax 831-667-2886.

In the Big Sur region, the only state-run campground de-signed to accommodate moderate-size (up to 32 feet) RVs is at **Pfeiffer Big Sur State Park**. Not only are the 218 tent/RV sites close to a grocery store, a restaurant, a gift shop and a laundromat, they're also right by the trailhead for the Pfeiffer Falls hiking trail, ideal for a romantic evening stroll. Sites have picnic tables and grills but no hookups. Campground facilities include restrooms with showers. Sites cost $25 to $31 per night. Open year-round. ~ Route 1, Big Sur; 831-667-2315, fax 831-667-2886; reservations 800-444-7275, www.reserveamerica.com.

For those who crave water and electric hookups, a stand-out among the privately operated RV parks in the Big Sur area is **Big Sur Campground and Cabins**. The setting is a shady redwood grove on the Big Sur River just a short distance from the restaurants and galleries of the Big Sur Valley. The camp-ground has 40 RV sites with hookups and 40 tent/RV sites with-

out hookups. Each site has a picnic table and grill, and there are restrooms, show-ers and a dump station as well as a kids' playground, a laundry room and a camping store. Sites cost $27 per night. Open year-round. ~ Route 1, Big Sur; 831-667-2322, fax 831-667-0456.

Big Sur Campground and Cabins.

Julia Pfeiffer Burns State Park has two small walk-in tent camping areas designed as backpacker base camps, each limited to eight people. Reservations required. Sites cost $25 to $31 per group of up to eight. Open year-round. ~ Route 1; 831-667-2315; reservations 800-444-7275, www.reserveamerica.com.

Cabin at Ripplewood Resort.

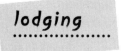
Lodging

The 13 cabins at **Big Sur Campground and Cabins** fall into three distinct categories. The tent cabins have canvas roofs and walls over wood frames; they're furnished and come with bedding and towels but share a central bathhouse. Several riverside "cabins" are actually mobile homes, well-kept with all the ambience you'd expect from trailer life. The newer A-frame cabins have contemporary mountain-style charm, with wood-burning stoves and sleeping lofts or separate bedrooms; some have full kitchens. ~Route 1, Big Sur; 831-667-2322, fax 831-667-0456. BUDGET TO DELUXE.

The 17 cabins at **Ripplewood Resort** range from small, plain units in redwood duplexes with carpeting, gas heaters and private baths but no kitchens to suite-sized cabins by the river with full kitchens, separate bedrooms and decks. ~ Route 1, Big Sur; 831-667-2242; www.ripplewoodresort.com. MODERATE.

Big Sur Lodge is set within Pfeiffer Big Sur State Park, close to the Pfeiffer Falls trailhead and an easy walk from a grocery store, gift shop, laundromat, restaurant and heated pool. Many of its 21 one-bedroom and 40 two-bedroom units are separate frame cottages with pine paneling, carpeting and beam ceilings. Each cottage has a kitchen, a fireplace and a porch or deck. ~ Route 1, Big Sur; 831-667-3100, 800-424-4787, fax 831-

667-3110; www.bigsurlodge.com, e-mail info@bigsurlodge.
com. DELUXE.

If room rates are not a concern, consider the rustic elegance
of the **Post Ranch Inn**. Set on the edge of a cliff, the inn's 30
separate wood-and-stone *casitas* include some that are set into
the hillside and covered with grass and others that stand on
stilts high above the forest floor. Each has a king-size bed and an
unobstructed view of the ocean or the redwoods, and is out-
fitted with a fireplace, hot tub and refrigerator. Complimentary
activities include daily yoga and nightly star gazing. Continental
breakfast included. Two-night minimum stay required. ~ Route
1, Big Sur; 831-667-2200, 800-527-2200, fax 831-667-2824; www.
postranchinn.com, e-mail info@postranchinn.com. ULTRA-
DELUXE.

The ultimate lodging in the Big Sur area, **Ventana Inn and
Spa** rambles across 243 acres of grounds on a mountain slope
overlooking the ocean. Showing just how luxurious a "rustic"

Post Ranch Inn.

• •

A Big Sur Classic

Best of that vanishing breed, the old-time bohemian lodges that helped give
Big Sur its unique character, **Deetjen's Big Sur Inn** is a haphazard jumble of

clapboard buildings with no locks on the doors.
The guest units are full of rustic charm, with
funky furnishings, throw rugs and local artwork,
but not much in the way of insulation. Some
have fireplaces, but there are no in-room
telephones or televisions. To call the inn's
atmosphere casual would be a profound under-
statement. ~ Route 1, Big Sur; 831-667-2377.
MODERATE TO ULTRA-DELUXE.

• •

lodge can be, the buildings are made of raw wood. Guest rooms
feature cedar paneling and handmade quilts. Lodge facilities
include two swimming pools, a fitness room, saunas, Japanese-
style hot baths, a clothing-optional sundeck and a library. The
room rates, ranging from $350 to nearly $1000 a night, include
wine and cheese and a continental breakfast. ~ Route 1, Big Sur;
831-667-2331, 800-628-6500, fax 831-667-2419; www.ventana
inn.com, e-mail reservations@ventanainn.com. ULTRA-DELUXE.

dining
• • • • • • • • • • • • •

A small local favorite serving dinner only, the **Bonito
Roadhouse** specializes in local seafood, though its
comprehensive menu also includes everything from
chicken pot pies to teriyaki steak. There's also a se-
lective list of fine central California wines. Reservations recommended. Closed Tuesdays. ~ Route 1, Big Sur; 831-667-
2264, fax 831-667-2865. MODERATE TO DELUXE.

Simplicity is the standard at **Fernwood**, a restaurant, bar
and general store that serves burgers, barbecued chicken,
homemade soup and chili for lunch or dinner. On the weekends, Fernwood hosts an outdoor barbecue with pork loin and
ribs. ~ Route 1, Big Sur; 831-667-2422, fax 831-667-2663.
BUDGET TO MODERATE.

The name means "heaven" in Spanish, and you'll see why
when you dine in the restaurant at **Cielo**, the restaurant in the
Ventana Inn. A spectacular sea view from either the indoor

Cielo restaurant at the Ventana Inn.

dining room or the broad veranda sets the stage for fine California cuisine, with a luncheon menu of steak sandwiches, premium fresh salads and tempting pasta dishes and a dinner menu featuring appetizers such as steamed artichokes and oysters on the half-shell and entrées including rack of lamb, filet mignon, quail and oak-grilled salmon. ~ Route 1, Big Sur; 831-667-2331, 800-628-6500, fax 831-667-2419; www.ventanainn.com. DE-LUXE TO ULTRA-DELUXE.

A true Big Sur legend, **Nepenthe** lures diners from Monterey and even San Francisco to rub elbows with everybody from Big Sur locals to celebrity visitors in a personality-packed indoor/outdoor setting 800 feet above the crashing surf. There's a selection of sandwiches, salads and quiches for lunch; dinner entrées include beef, fowl and seafood dishes. ~ Route 1, Big Sur; 831-667-2345, fax 831-667-2394; www.nepenthebigsur.com. MODERATE TO DELUXE.

Nepenthe.

••

Cuisine with a View

Sierra Mar, the restaurant at the Post Ranch Inn, boasts a view from a clifftop
1100 feet above the ocean shore, making a sunset dinner an unforgettable experience. The prix-fixe menu changes daily and focuses on healthy choices made with
the freshest ingredients, including catch-of-the-day seafood and lean beef along
with vegetables from the inn's own gardens. Dinner only. ~ Route 1, Big Sur; 831-
667-2800, fax 831-667-2824; www.postranchinn.com. ULTRA-DELUXE.

••

Downstairs from Nepenthe and under the same management, open-air **Café Kevah** serves egg dishes, waffles and
homemade pastries for breakfast and Mexican fare for lunch.
The prices are considerably lower than Nepenthe's and the sea
view is every bit as magnificent. Closed in January and February
and during inclement weather. ~ Route 1, Big Sur; 831-667-
2345, fax 831-667-2394; www.nepenthebigsur.com. BUDGET TO
MODERATE.

nightlife

At the **Big Sur River Inn**, a comfortable wood-
paneled bar above the Big Sur River has live Dixie-
land jazz on Sunday afternoons. ~ Route 1; 831-
667-2700, 800-548-3610; www.bigsurriverinn.com.

You'll also find cocktail lounges at some of the more upscale resorts such as the **Ventana Inn**. ~ Route 1, Big Sur; 831-
667-2331, 800-628-6500; www.ventanainn.com.

Otherwise, any nightlife you find around Big Sur is likely
to be of the four-legged variety.

index

....

lodging & dining index

HIDDEN GUIDES

Adventure travel or a relaxing vacation?—"Hidden" guidebooks are the only travel books in the business to provide detailed information on both. Aimed at environmentally aware travelers, our motto is "Where Vacations Meet Adventures." These books combine details on unique hotels, restaurants and sightseeing with information on camping, sports and hiking for the outdoor enthusiast.

THE NEW KEY GUIDES

Based on the concept of ecotourism, The New Key Guides are dedicated to the preservation of Central America's rare and endangered species, architecture and archaeology. Filled with helpful tips, they give travelers everything they need to know about these exotic destinations.

HIDDEN GUIDEBOOKS

____ Hidden Arizona, $16.95
____ Hidden Bahamas, $14.95
____ Hidden Baja, $14.95
____ Hidden Belize, $15.95
____ Hidden Big Island of Hawaii, $13.95
____ Hidden Boston & Cape Cod, $14.95
____ Hidden British Columbia, $18.95
____ Hidden Cancún & the Yucatán, $16.95
____ Hidden Carolinas, $17.95
____ Hidden Coast of California, $18.95
____ Hidden Colorado, $15.95
____ Hidden Disneyland, $13.95
____ Hidden Florida, $18.95
____ Hidden Florida Keys & Everglades, $13.95
____ Hidden Georgia, $16.95
____ Hidden Guatemala, $16.95
____ Hidden Hawaii, $18.95
____ Hidden Idaho, $14.95

____ Hidden Kauai, $13.95
____ Hidden Maui, $13.95
____ Hidden Montana, $15.95
____ Hidden New England, $18.95
____ Hidden New Mexico, $15.95
____ Hidden Oahu, $13.95
____ Hidden Oregon, $15.95
____ Hidden Pacific Northwest, $18.95
____ Hidden Salt Lake City, $14.95
____ Hidden San Francisco & Northern California, $18.95
____ Hidden Southern California, $18.95
____ Hidden Southwest, $19.95
____ Hidden Tahiti, $17.95
____ Hidden Tennessee, $16.95
____ Hidden Utah, $16.95
____ Hidden Walt Disney World, $13.95
____ Hidden Washington, $15.95
____ Hidden Wine Country, $13.95
____ Hidden Wyoming, $15.95

NEW KEY GUIDEBOOKS

____ The New Key to Costa Rica, $18.95

____ The New Key to Ecuador and the Galápagos, $17.95

Mark the book(s) you're ordering and enter the total cost here ➥ _____

California residents add 8.25% sales tax here ➥ _____

Shipping, check box for your preferred method and enter cost here ➥ _____

❑ BOOK RATE   **FREE! FREE! FREE!**

❑ PRIORITY MAIL/UPS GROUND   cost of postage

❑ UPS OVERNIGHT OR 2-DAY AIR   cost of postage   _____

Billing, enter total amount due and check method of payment ➥ _____

❑ CHECK   ❑ MONEY ORDER

❑ VISA/MASTERCARD EXP. DATE

NAME _____ PHONE _____

ADDRESS _____

CITY _____ STATE _____ ZIP _____

MONEY-BACK GUARANTEE ON DIRECT ORDERS PLACED THROUGH ULYSSES PRESS.

about the author

Richard Harris has written or co-written 31 other guidebooks including Ulysses' *Weekend Adventure Getaways: Yosemite Tahoe*; *Hidden Baja*; *Hidden Cancún and the Yucatán* and the bestselling *Hidden Southwest*. He has also served as contributing editor on guides to Mexico, New Mexico, and other ports of call for John Muir Publications, Fodor's, Birnbaum and Access guides. He is a past president of PEN New Mexico and currently president of the New Mexico Book Association. When not traveling, Richard writes and lives in Santa Fe, New Mexico.

about the photographer

Lee Foster is a travel photographer/writer based in Berkeley, California. Lee's website (www.fostertravel.com) presents over 200 worldwide destinations, including his speciality, Northern California. His most recent book is *Northern California History Weekends* (Globe Pequot). Lee provides travel photos and writing for major print publications, from *Travel & Leisure* to the *New York Times*. He has won seven Lowell Thomas Awards, the highest awards in travel journalism, and has been named Lowell Thomas Travel Journalist of the Year, Silver Winner.